Test Your
C++ Skills

Yashavant P. Kanetkar

BPB PUBLICATIONS
B-14, CONNAUGHT PLACE, NEW DELHI-1

FIRST EDITION 2002 REPRINTED 2005

Distributors:

MICRO BOOK CENTRE
2, City Centre, CG Road,
Near Swastic Char Rasta,
AHMEDABAD-380009 Phone: 26421611

COMPUTER BOOK CENTRE
12, Shrungar Shopping Centre, M.G. Road,
BANGALORE-560001 Phone: 5587923, 5584641

MICRO BOOKS
Shanti Niketan Building, 8, Camac Street,
KOLKATTA-700017 Phone: 22826518, 22826519

BUSINESS PROMOTION BUREAU
8/1, Ritchie Street, Mount Road,
CHENNAI-600002 Phone: 28410796, 28550491

DECCAN AGENCIES
4-3-329, Bank Street,
HYDERABAD-500195 Phone: 24756400, 24756967

MICRO MEDIA
Shop No. 5, Mahendra Chambers, 150 D.N. Road,
Next to Capital Cinema V.T. (C.S.T.) Station,
MUMBAI-400001 Ph.: 22078296, 22078297

BPB PUBLICATIONS
B-14, Connaught Place, **NEW DELHI-110001**
Phone: 23325760, 23723393, 23737742

INFOTECH
G-2, Sidhartha Building, 96 Nehru Place,
NEW DELHI-110019
Phone: 26438245, 26415092, 26234208

INFOTECH
Shop No. 2, F-38, South Extension Part-1
NEW DELHI-110049
Phone: 24691288, 24641941

BPB BOOK CENTRE
376, Old Lajpat Rai Market,
DELHI-110006 PHONE: 23861747

Price : Rs. 180/-

ISBN 81-7656-554-7

Published by Manish Jain for BPB Publications, B-14, Connaught Place, New Delhi-110 001 and Printed by him at Pressworks, Delhi.

Dedicated to
Prabhakar Kanetkar

About the Author

Yashavant Prabhakar Kanetkar obtained his B.E. from VJTI Bombay and his M. Tech. from IIT Kanpur. A Mechanical Engineer by education, he switched to computers a decade ago and hasn't looked back since. Mr. Kanetkar is author of several books including Let Us C, Exploring C, C Projects, Understanding Pointers In C, Unix Shell Programming, Visual C++ Projects, published by BPB Publications and Tech Publications, Singapore. Today Yashavant divides his working hours among writing articles for Express Computer, writing books, teaching classes and conducting training seminars in C/C++/VC++. Since 1987 he has been Director of KICIT, a Training firm which he set up at Nagpur.

Acknowledgments

While framing questions it must be made absolutely sure that they are pin-pointing and have no ambiguity whatsoever. While answering questions one has to strike a delicate balance between being to the point yet elaborate. Vineeta Prasad and Anil Gakhare showed exemplary patience and willingness to get it right. Their dedication in poring through source code and struggling through complex explanations inspired me to keep pushing hard to make this book better. It is a delight to work with and learn from such a talented group of programmers.

Thanks to Shakeel for another heroic effort. Be it technical assistance on wide-ranging topics, or management of numerous projects including this one, Shakeel does it with effortless ease. His hard work and courteous professionalism go beyond the call of duty.

A mechanical engineer by education, a marketing manger by experience is now wetting his feet in C++. It all speaks about an open mind. And Rajiv Parkhi has that in abundance, as he once again proved with his contribution to this book project.

It is said that one learns best when one is teaching. I have been no exception to this rule. I have learnt the intricacies of this language while teaching C++ to numerous students all over the country. Many thanks to all of you!

Above all, thanks to my family, who understand the demands of a normal business but gave up far more because of this book. I want to remain in their debt.

And, of course, the entire crew at KICIT. They provide so much insight, ideas, motivation, and inspiration and are so much fun to work with! Thanks!

Contents

Interview with Dr. P. J. Plauger, the C++ guru

 Dr. P.J. Plauger is a well-known name in the C/C++ world with a long list of accomplishments. He has earned a Ph.D. in nuclear physics, has worked at Bell Labs (in the early days of Unix), and has founded two software companies Whitesmiths, Ltd., and Dinkumware, Ltd. He has been active in the development of international standards, most notably for the programming languages C and C++. Until recently, he was Senior Editor of The C/C++ Users Journal and Contributing Editor to Embedded Systems Programming.

Given the rich experience that Plauger has in conceiving and handling programming projects of all sizes I asked him about his personal approach to a programming project. In Plauger's words, "First I envision my final goal, then I identify a series of small steps that lead toward that goal. Each step must result in executable code that I can test."

When I asked him what are the new challenges that a C++ programmer should be prepared to face, this is what he opined. "C++ has grown so much in the process of standardization that it now contains many gray areas, where compilers do different (and sometimes erroneous) things. It's hard to learn a powerful yet portable subset of the language and library."

Plauger offers this advice to budding C++ programmers, "Learn the simple stuff well first, before trying the fancy stuff." Given Plauger's experience with the C++ language, there is evidently truth in this statement.

Since Plauger has been involved in programming since early sixties and has seen it all I asked him about his thoughts about other programming languages. In his opinion, "No one language is perfect for all jobs, so you must avoid the temptation to adapt all problems to suit the limitations of your favorite language."

Plauger's motto of programming is simple and appealing, "I love programming, and I make good money at it." This I believe echoes the feelings of all hardcore C++ programmers.

This is what he has to say about his current work—"Now that, Dinkumware, has established itself as the leading supplier of Standard C and C++ libraries, we're fleshing out the sketchier parts of both libraries, such as support for alternate locales and character sets, portable support for multithreading, etc." He also stresses the importance of bringing many compiler vendors who still need to be brought up to date with C/C++ library conformance.

What drives him to creative programming is best described in his words, "I accept that I will not always be highly productive week in and week out." So simple, yet so true.

Plauger lives with his family in Concord, Massachusetts. When he is not working he attends many plays, operas, and concerts. Occasionally he also indulges in writing science fiction.

Introduction

This book is not intended to be a text-book of C++ programming. There are several other texts that can address this need. I felt there is a need for a book that would help reader test his skills and understanding of the C++ language. Hence, this book follows a question and answer format rather than an encyclopedic coverage of each topic. Each question in the book is meant to illustrate a single idea relevant to the question. Though I have attempted to address every facet of a topic by cooking suitable questions it would be too much to expect that this book would contain answer to every one of your queries. This is due to the fact that many questions that may come up in your programming practice may have to do something with the problem domain rather than a language feature.

The book assumes that you are familiar with the basic language elements like variables, functions and control instructions. The questions is this book are the product of several years of teaching others to use C++ effectively, as well as several discussions with fellow C++ programmers at KICIT.

I have made an effort to ensure that most of the programs in the book are complete runnable programs rather than mere code snippets. All the programs in this book have been tested under Visual C++ 6.0 under windows. You may try them with other compilers as well.

The questions in each chapter deal with a specific topic. They have been arranged in increasing order of complexity. Immediately after the question you will find the answer to it and a brief explanation about why that is the answer. Some answers have been purposefully made more elaborate than the others. This has been done with a motive to give you a complete picture rather than oversimplifying things or leaving out important details.

A hidden agenda of this book is to change the way you think about the language and its utility in solving problems rather than merely teaching you the language syntax. If you have the patience to go through all the questions I am hopeful that this purpose of the book would be served.

Intro to OOP

Q 1.1

I keep hearing that in structured programming data is given a step-motherly treatment and the whole emphasis is on doing things. What does this mean in programmer's language?

Ans

Structured programming languages like C and Pascal define data structures (arrays, structures, unions, enums, etc.) and provide functions that inspect or change the data form any place in the program. When the program grows beyond a reasonable size it becomes unmanageable since the data structures are available throughout the program and changing them in one part may have repercussions on other part of the program.

Object-oriented programming reduces dependencies between different parts of a program. An object contains data structures and a set of operations for inspecting and manipulating them. All operations that require the knowledge of data structures are directly associated with the structures, rather than being spread throughout the program. Combining the data and the operations that inspect and modify the data brings in huge benefits. This arrangement ensures that you do not directly manipulate the data, instead you request functions associated with the data to do this job for you. Thus, part of the program that requests action to be performed on the data structures remains separate from the part which fulfills the request. As a result, now the parts of the program do not depend on each other through the data structures but through the functionality that the parts promise to provide. When you approach a programming problem in an object-oriented language you do not ask how the problem will be divided into functions. Instead you ask how it will be divided into objects.

Q 1.2

Can you explain to me the difference between classes and objects in layman's terms?

Ans

A class is a blueprint for objects. From one class several objects can be created. Each object is known as an instance of a particular class. For example, 'Cricketers' is a class, whereas, 'Sachin', 'Saurav', 'Rahul' are specific instances of the 'Cricketers' class (hence they are objects). The blueprint for 'Cricketers' class describes how a cricketer would look like (colored/white clothing, cap, shoes, etc.) and what operations can he perform (bat, bowl, field, etc.). Similarly, you can imagine 'Musicians' as a class and 'Lata' and 'Asha' as specific instances of this class. Again, from one class of musicians several instances (objects) can be created.

Q 1.3

Can you explain to me the difference between classes and objects in programmer's terms?

Ans

In the simplest terms in *int i*, *int* is a *class* and *i* is an object of that *class*. From the *int class* we can create several objects (variables). The *int* class indicates what kind of data an object of its type can hold and what operations (addition, subtraction, etc.) can be performed on this data. A class is thus a description of number of similar objects. It specifies what data and what functions will be included in objects of that class.

Instead of standard class like *int* you can think of user-defined class like *employee* from which objects like, *e1*, *e2*, *e3* can be created through a statement,

employee e1, e2, e3 ;

Q 1.4

Can you give me a few examples that will help me to appreciate the difference between a class and an object?

Ans

Class	Object
Human Being	Anil, Sunil, etc.
Bird	Sparrow, Eagle, etc.
Reptile	Snakes, Tortoise, etc.

Complex Number	3.5 + 7i, 2.6 – 4i, etc.
Car	Corsa, Accent, etc.
User-Interface element	Menu, Toolbar, etc.
Shape	Line, Rectangle, etc.
Complete Hardware	Mouse, Keyboard, Printer, etc.
Air-traffic Control system	Aeroplanes, Airports

Q 1.5

What do you mean by encapsulation?

Ans

Encapsulation is the mechanism that binds together the code and data it manipulates, and keeps both safe from outside interference and misuse. The advantage of encapsulated code is that the outside world knows how to access it and thus can use it regardless of the implementation details and without fear of unexpected side-effects. In C++ the basis of encapsulation is a *class*. The purpose of a *class* is to encapsulate complexity and C++ provides mechanisms for hiding the complexity of implementation inside the *class*.

Q 1.6

What is Inheritance?

Ans

Inheritance is a process of creating new classes, called *derived classes* from existing or *base classes*. The derived class inherits all the capabilities of the base class and can either refine some of its features or add totally new features of its own. This relationship is shown in the following figure.

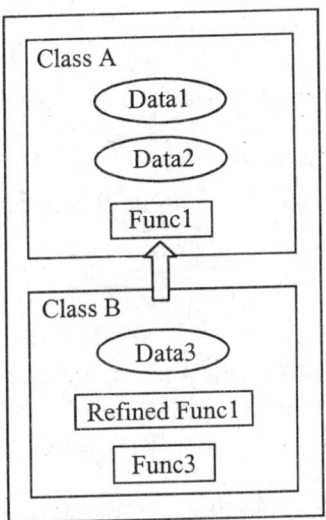

Inheritance works the same way as in real-life. Children inherit features from their parents, refine some of them and add a few of their own.

Q 1.7

What is polymorphism?

Ans

Polymorphism means the ability to assume several forms. In object-oriented programming context this refers to the ability of an entity to refer to objects of various classes at runtime.

C++ has three mechanisms that help us to implement polymorphism. These are:

– Function overloading
– Operator overloading

– Virtual functions

These mechanisms are discussed at length in chapters to come.

Q 1.8

In real life do I encounter situations where an interface is separated from its implementation?

Ans

Frequently. For example to shift gears of a gearbox in an automobile the interface is always the gear lever. However, the implementation of the gearbox may vastly change from one automobile to another.

An interface to supply text to a computer is always the keys on the keyboard. The implementation of these keys however might be mechanical in one keyboard and capacitor-based in another.

Q 1.9

What is the advantage of separating an interface from its implementation?

Ans

If the implementation remains separate from an interface we can have the flexibility of changing the implementation. New technologies like Component Object Model (COM), Enterprise Java Beans (EJB) are based on this facet of object-oriented programming.

Q 1.10

What is the difference between an object-based language and an object-oriented language?

Ans

Languages that support only objects and classes are called object-based languages. Such languages do not support features like inheritance and polymorphism. They merely let you create objects and call methods using these objects.

Q 1.11

What is the basic difference between Visual Basic and Visual C++?

Ans

Visual Basic is an object-based language, whereas, Visual C++ is an object-oriented language.

Q 1.12

Inspite of so many object-oriented languages available, why did C++ become more popular?

Ans

To a large extent C++ has backward compatibility with C. While converting existing system to object-oriented system this became an important parameter. As transformation to an object-oriented system is usually done a few subsystems at a time, it was important to ensure that existing C code worked in tandem with new C++ code. The C++ compiler could compile the older C code thereby ensuring that non-object-oriented subsystems could coexist with the new object-oriented subsystems.

Also, while shifting to C++, the C programmers found the learning curve smoother than shifting to a completely new object-oriented language.

Q 1.13

Is it appropriate to call C++ as 'better C'?

Ans

Never commit that mistake. If you do so you would miss out on most of the benefits that object-oriented programming brings about. It is important that you change your mind-set from structured programming to object-oriented programming with C++ as a vehicle to do so. If you don't do this you would end up writing C programs in C++.

Q 1.14

What do you mean by abstraction?

Ans

In layman's language abstraction tells users everything that they may want to know about an object and nothing else. In C++ language an abstraction indicates what data can an object hold and what functions can it perform on the data. How these functions are performed is abstracted away. For example, a stack may be viewed as an abstraction. The stack can be understood and used once we come to know the features like push and pop that it provides, without bothering about how it stores the data or how the push and pop operations are performed.

Q 1.15

What does it take to build good abstractions?

Ans

Unless you have good domain knowledge of the problem you are trying to solve, you would not be able to create good abstractions.

Q 1.16

Is it necessary to create good abstractions?

Ans

Absolutely. A properly created abstraction lets the user use an object in a safe and predictable manner. A good abstraction separates specification from implementation. In fact the abstraction should be so good that a user should never be tempted to look at the implementation of the object.

Q 1.17

What is the purpose of inheritance?

Ans

The basic purpose of inheritance is to extend the capability of an entity by inheriting from an existing entity. It works the same way as in the real-world scenario: children inherit the features from their parents.

Q 1.18

What is the purpose of polymorphism?

Ans

The purpose of polymorphism is to provide a way for an entity to behave in several forms. For example, the same gear lever can be used to move the car forward or backward.

Q 1.19

What is a class and what is an object?

Ans

A class is a design. Object is the creation from this design. Multiple objects can be created from a single class. The class defines the type of object that can be created according to the data the object can hold and the operations the object can perform.

Q 1.20

Why did people change over from structured programming to object-oriented programming?

Ans

When a program designed using the structured programming paradigm grows beyond a certain limit it becomes unmanageable on two counts:

(a) The program does not have enough flexibility to meet the rapidly changing demands of a typical business environment. This is because even a well-designed structured system does not have much scope for reusing its existing subsystems in future to meet the changing business requirements. Even in well-designed structured systems enhancements often require modifications to significant portions of existing design and code. As against this, object-oriented programming systems permit reuse of existing code through features like inheritance, polymorphism and dynamic-binding.

(b) The software built around structured programming paradigm is difficult to maintain, especially so when the person maintaining the program is not from the original development team.

COMBATING MENACE OF PIRACY

Dear Readers, Publishers, Booksellers, all College & University Administrations, & Librarians,

The Federation of Publishers' & Book Sellers' Associations in India (FPBAI) would like to bring a matter of great importance to your urgent notice. Though possession of pirated copies is a cognizable and non-bailable offence, punishable by law and carries stiff penalties including imprisonment, it continues to thrive in markets, bookshops and photocopy shops. This is a matter of grave concern for all of us in the education and publishing community. Let us all do our bit in combating this crime against creation and spread of knowledge. If you come across a pirated book, photocopies pages from a book or are in any kind of doubt about the genuineness of a copy, please contact Chairman, Anti Piracy Committee, FPBAI, 84, Second Floor (Opp. Cambridge Primary School), Daryaganj, New Delhi-110 002.

Your co-operation and help in bringing the culprits to book will help the publishing industry combat piracy and facilitate the continued availability of good books of quality production at reasonable prices.

RELEVANT PORTIONS OF THE COPYRIGHT ACT ARE GIVEN BELOW:

INFRINGEMENT OF COPYRIGHT

The owner of the copyright has the exclusive right in respect of the reproduction of the work and such other acts which enables the owner to get the financial benefits by exercising such rights. If any of these acts relating to the work is carried out by a person other than the owner without a license from the owner or competent person/authority under the Copyright Act 1957, it constitutes infringement of copyright in the work.

PIRACY

It is a kind of illegal activity which has been caused by rapid technological advancement. Latest techniques of photocopying and printing have made it easy to produce unauthorized copies of a book within a short span of time at a relatively low cost on a large scale. This offence deprives the author of the work from getting his legitimate due and ultimately hampers the growth of original and creative work by the pursuit of hard work and intellectual skill and national economy as well.

COPYRIGHT LEGISLATION

The Principal Act (Copyright Act, 1957) was amended in 1984 to incorporate anti-piracy legislation to check widespread piracy of books, etc. and it has been made a cognizable and non-bailable offence.

The punishment for various offences have been enhanced by amending sections 63 and 65 and by inserting new sections 63A & 63B.

SECTION 63:

Any person who knowingly infringes or abets the infringement of the copyright work shall be punishable with:

    (i)   Imprisonment for a term which shall not be less than 6 months but which may be extended up to 3 years;

    (ii)   Fine of not less than Rs. 50,000/- but up to Rs. 2 lakhs.

SECTION 63A:

The quantum of enhanced penalty on second or subsequent conviction shall be:

    (i)   Imprisonment for not less than 1 year but up to 3 years; and

    (ii)   Fine of not less than rupees 1 lakh but may be extended up to Rs. 2 lakhs.

SECTION 63B:

The quantum penalty for the offence of knowing use of infringing copy of computer program shall be:

    (i)   Imprisonment for not less than 7 days but up to 3 years; and

    (ii)   Fine of not less than Rs. 50,000/- but may be extended up to Rs. 2 lakhs.

More powers have been given to the police for prompt action and speedy apprehension of the offender by amending section 64, as any police officer not below the rank of Sub-Inspector may seize without warrant all infringing copies or the work if he is satisfied that the offence is under section 63 in respect of the infringement of copyright. The Economic Offence (Inapplicability of Limitation) Act, 1974 was amended by incorporating in the Schedule the clause (a) of section 63 of the Copyright Act, 1957 which declared infringement of copyright as an economic offence.

Graduating To C++

Q 2.1

What is the advantage of C++ being a block-structured language?

Ans

We know memory is always at a premium. In block structured programming we can save memory by controlling the life of variables. For example, consider the following function:

```
void fun( )
{
    // 20 statements
    {
        int a ;
        // statement using a
    }
    // 100 more statements
}
```

Here *a* has been defined inside a block as it is not needed once the control passes the block. As soon as the control goes outside the block *a* dies thereby freeing the memory occupied by it. Had *a* been defined at the beginning of the function, *a* would have survived till execution of the function had not come to an end.

Q 2.2

How is the *int* data type different than *short* and *long* data types?

Ans

The *short* and *long* occupy 2 and 4 bytes respectively regardless of the underlying OS. On the other hand an *int* occupies 2 bytes under DOS and 4 bytes under Windows. This results into better performance. For example, if the program is running under Windows then the *int* variable can store value more than 32767. If this program runs under DOS the value would be wrapped on the negative side giving wrong results. At such times we can use a *long*. But *long* being 4-byte entity degrades the program's performance under DOS because DOS is a 16-bit OS. The same applies for *short* under Windows, which is a 32-bit OS. But *int* gives better performance regardless of the OS because it gets modified according to the OS.

Q 2.3

Do function declarations get stored in an EXE file?

Ans

No. The compiler uses function declarations for proper compilation. Once the program is compiled they are not required, hence are prevented from getting added into the EXE file.

Q 2.4

When should the function declarations be made global?

Ans

The function declarations should be made global when the function being declared is called from more than one function.

Q 2.5

Why nested comments are not allowed?

Ans

Consider the following example:

/* This is a comment /*Nested comments */ are not allowed. */

Anything that lies between /* and */ is treated as a comment. In the above example from "This" up to "comments" everything is treated as comment including "/*". Hence "are not allowed. */" does not lie in the comment. This being an improper C statement error occurs.

Q 2.6

Is this a valid C++ comment?

// This is an /* invalid */ comment

Ans

Yes. Whatever lies in the line after // is treated as comment. Since /* invalid */ lies in the same line after //, it is treated as part of the comment.

Q 2.7

What is an anonymous *union*? What are the restrictions imposed on an anonymous *union*?

Ans

An anonymous *union* does not have a *union* name (tag), and its elements can be accessed directly without using a *union* variable. Simply omitting the *union* name in the declaration does not make the *union* an anonymous *union*. For a *union* to qualify as an anonymous *union*, the declaration must not declare a variable of the *union* type.

Anonymous *union*s are subject to additional restrictions:

– When declared globally they must be *static*.
– Their elements can be *public*, they cannot be *private* or *protected*.
– Member functions within them are not allowed.

Q 2.8

Would the following statements work?

```
void *p ;
float *q ;
int *r ;
p = q ;
p = r ;
```

Ans

There is no need to typecast a pointer when it is assigned to a *void* pointer. But it is necessary to typecast a *void* pointer when it is assigned to any other type.

```
void *p ;
int *i ;
p = i ; // correct
i = p ; // error
```

Q 2.9

What does the following prototype indicate:

const char *fun (char const*, const char *) ;

Ans .

const char *fun (char const*, const char *) ;

This prototype indicates that the function *fun( )* receives two parameters of type pointer to a constant string and returns a pointer to a constant string. Also refer Q 2.25.

Q 2.10

When should we make a call by reference?

Ans

A call by pointer or a call by reference is useful in two situations:

(a) When we intend to change the values of actual arguments through the called function.

(b) When we want to save memory by preventing the creation of large structure variables that are being passed to the function.

To achieve these purposes references offer a cleaner and more elegant way as compared to pointers, as with references, we are not required to use the * and -> operators.

Q 2.11

What are the advantages of *cout* and *cin* over *printf( )* and *scanf( )*?

Ans

With *cout* and *cin* we are not required to give format specifiers (%d, %f, %c, etc.). *cin* and *cout* being objects we can use operator overloading to make them work even with the user-defined data types.

Q 2.12

Is reference a pointer?

Ans

A reference is a *const* pointer. Hence once initialized a reference cannot be made to refer to another variable. Unlike a pointer a reference gets automatically de-referenced.

Q 2.13

Is reference to a reference allowed?

Ans

No. Because when we try to assign a reference to a reference the new reference starts referring to the same variable the first reference is referring to.

```
int i ;
int &j = i ;
int &k = j ; // reference to a reference.
```

Here, *k* is a reference to a reference *j* and both *j* and *k* refer to the variable *i*.

Q 2.14

Can we create a pointer to a reference?

Ans

No. This can be explained with the help of following code:

```
int i ;
int &p = i ;
int *j = &p ;  // not a pointer to a reference
```

Here it seems that *j* is a pointer to the reference *p*, but actually it is pointing to the variable *i*. This is because a reference is automatically de-referenced, i.e., *&p* internally becomes *&**p. Thus in *j* what gets stored is address of *i*.

Q 2.15

Why is using *const* a better idea than an equivalent *#define*?

Ans

Using *const* is always a better idea as compared to *#define* because while using *const* we can control its scope of operation by placing it either inside a function or outside all functions. If it is placed inside a function its effect would be localized to that function, whereas, if it is placed outside all functions then its effect would be global. We cannot exercise such finer control while using *#define*.

Q 2.16

How would the compiler interpret the following statements?

```
int i = 9 ;
int &p = i ;
int &q = p ;
```

Ans

The compiler would interpret the statements as shown below.

```
int  i = 9 ;
int  * const p = &i ;
int  * const q = &*p ;
```

As a reference is nothing but a *const* pointer the address of the variable gets stored in a reference. Hence in the second statement address of *i* gets stored in *const* pointer *p*. And as references are automatically de-referenced *p* becomes *& *p* in the third statement.

Q 2.17

What are the advantages of references over pointers?

Ans

While using pointers we have to explicitly de-reference the pointer by using 'value at address' operator (*). But while using references we don't have to use 'value at address' operator since a reference gets automatically de-referenced. Thus references are cleaner and more elegant as compared to pointers. Also, if we want the change being made in the parameter in the called function to become effective in the calling function, we shall make a call by reference as it avoids copying of the variable.

Q 2.18

If *employee* is a structure, *REGS* is a union and *maritalstatus* is an enum then does there exist any other way in which the following definitions can be made:

```
struct employee e ;
union REGS i ;
enum maritalstatus m ;
```

Ans

```
employee e ;
REGS i ;
```

maritalstatus m ;

Q 2.19

What are the advantages of pointers over references?

Ans

Reference being a *const* pointer cannot be reassigned. On the other hand pointers can be reassigned. This is shown in the following example:

```
main( )
{
    int i, j ;
    int *p = &i ;
    p = &j ;
}
```

Also, arithmetic operations cannot be performed on a reference. This is shown in the following example:

```
main( )
{
    int i ;
    int &r = i ;
    r++ ;
    int *p = &i ;
    p++ ;
}
```

Here $r++$ would not increment the value of r. But it will increment value of i. This means that when an arithmetic operation is performed on a reference, it gets performed on a referent. But when $p++$ is done, the value of p is incremented.

Q 2.20

Why should we not return a reference or an address of a local variable?

Ans

When we return a reference to a local variable, the variable would die once control returns to the calling function. Hence, calling function would be referring to a variable that no longer exists.

Q 2.21

Can we have a *const* reference and where do we need such a type?

Ans

Yes, we can have a *const* reference. Passing a variable to a function by reference is a better idea as compared to passing it by value because it prevents a new variable from getting created. But when we do so there is a possibility that the variable may get modified in the function accidentally. This can be prevented by declaring it as *const*.

Q 2.22

Can we create a reference to an array?

Ans

Yes, a reference to an array is allowed. For example:

```
int a[ ] = { 3, 7, 6, 9, 5 } ;
int (&p)[ 5 ] = a ;  // reference to an array
```

Q 2.23

Why is it so that when we print the address of a reference the address of a referent gets printed?

Ans

References are always automatically de-referenced. So when we print the address of the reference the address of the referent gets printed. For example:

```
int i;
int &r = i;
```

When we write &*r* it is actually treated as &**r* which is nothing but address of the value stored in *r*, that is address of *i*.

Q 2.24

Do the following code segments perform the same job:

(a)   int a = 10;

     int a (10);

     Ans

     Yes. In C++ all intrinsic types are treated as classes. The *int a (10)* is another type of initialization which is allowed for the variables (objects) of a class. This is known as class constructor notation.

(b)   bool a;

     BOOL a;

     Ans

     No. *bool* is a keyword but BOOL is not.

(c)   cout << "\n";

```
cout << '\n' ;
cout << endl ;
```

Ans

Yes. All the three statements perform the same job of placing the cursor in the next line. *endl* is a manipulator which inserts a linefeed in the output stream.

(d)   enum grade g ;

       grade g ;

Ans

Yes. In C++ *struct, class, union* or *enum* keywords are optional while defining a variable (object) of that type. This is allowed to maintain the consistency between user-defined data types and intrinsic data types.

(e)   void f (int x, float y) ;

       void f (int , float) ;

Ans

Yes. Mentioning the variable names in the function declaration is optional.

Q 2.25

In the following code fragment which is constant, the pointer or the string?

(a)   char *p = "Nagpur" ;

(b)   const char *q = "Nagpur" ;

(c)   char const *r = "Nagpur" ;

(d)   char * const s = "Nagpur" ;

(e) const char * const t = "Nagpur" ;

Ans

(a) Pointer and string both are variable. For example:

```
char *p = "Nagpur" ;
*p = 'K' ; // works
p = "KICIT" ; // works
```

(b) String is constant but pointer is not. For example:

```
const char *q = "Nagpur" ;
*q = 'K' ; // error
q = "KICIT" ; // works
```

(c) String is constant but pointer is not. For example:

```
char const *r = "Nagpur" ·
*r = 'K' ; // error
r = "KICIT" ; // works
```

(d) Pointer is constant but string is not. For example:

```
char * const  s = "Nagpur" ;
*s = 'K' ; // Works
s = "KICIT" ; // error
```

(e) String and pointer both are constant. For example:

```
const char * const  t = "Nagpur" ;
*t = 'K' ; // error
t = "KICIT" ; // error
```

Q 2.26

State whether the following statements are True or False:

(a) In C++ re-definition of variables is not allowed whereas re-declaration is allowed.

Ans

True. We know that the life and scope of a variable exists within the block in which it is defined. In the following example:

```
void main( )
{
    int a ;
    int a ;  // redefinition
    a = 10 ;
}
```

We are trying to define the variable *a* twice within the same block. But when *a* is assigned a value 10, compiler would fail to decide which *a* to use. Hence, redefinition is not allowed.

On the other hand re-declaration is allowed because merely declaring a variable does not occupy any space in memory. It is just an instruction given to compiler that at some stage in later part of the program the variable is defined. For example:

```
fun( )
{
    extern int i ;
    extern int i ; // re-declaration
}

int i ;
```

Here, *extern int i* is merely a declaration of variable *i* which is defined after the function *fun( )*.

(b) In C++ a union can contain data members as well as member functions.

Ans

True. C++ being an object-oriented language facilitates data encapsulation. Hence, data may not be freely accessible from outside the union. To allow data access functions can be provided inside the union.

(c) If a function is defined before calling it, there is no need to mention its prototype.

Ans

True. When compiler encounters a function call it needs information (like name of the function, number of arguments, types of arguments, order of arguments and default values) about the function for proper compilation. This information is available even in the function definition. Hence there is no need of function declaration if the definition is written before the call. This is shown in the following example:

```
#include <iostream.h>

void fun ( int i ) // Function definition.
{
    cout << "In function fun." ;
}

void main( )
{
    fun ( 5 );
}
```

(d) A reference is internally treated as a *const* pointer.

Ans

True. Once a reference start pointing to a particular variable it cannot be made to point to another variable. Thus it is a *const* pointer.

(e) It is possible to create an array of references.

Ans

False. A reference is not an object. Hence we cannot find address of a reference, nor can we create an array of references.

(f) Once a reference is tied with a variable it cannot be tied with another variable.

Ans

True. A reference being a *const* pointer, once initialized its value cannot be changed.

(g) A reference cannot be reinitialized.

Ans

True. Explanation – same as (e) above.

(h) A variable can be tied with several references.

Ans

True. This is because there is no limitation on storing the address of a variable in multiple pointers. Since references are *const* pointers this works. For example:

```
int  a = 10 ;
int  &b = a ;
int  &c = a ;
```

(i) In C++ a function call can occur even on the left-hand side of an assignment operator.

Ans

True. If a function returns a reference its call can exist on the left-hand side of an assignment operator. This is shown in the following code:

```
#include <iostream.h>

int i ;
void main( )
{
    int &fun( ) ;
    fun( ) = 10 ;
    cout << i ;
}

int &fun( )
{
    i = 2 ;
    return i ;
}
```

Here, the function *fun( )* returns a reference to an integer variable *i*. The returned reference replaces the function call, Hence the statement becomes *(reference of i) = 10*. Hence *i* would be assigned a value 10, as can be verified by output of *cout*.

(j) It is unsafe to return a local variable by reference.

Ans

True. As soon as the function returns, local variables die. If a reference (or address) of a local variable is returned, it means we would be referring to the dead variable.

(k) *cin* and *cout* are objects.

Ans

True. *cin* and *cout* are objects of classes *istream_withassign* and *ostream_withassign* respectively. They are not implemented as intrinsic data types. They are defined in the file "iostream.h".

(l) C++ permits the use of anonymous structures.

Ans

True. Anonymous structure means the structure that does not have any name. Such a structure is created when it is not required at other places. This is shown in the following code:

```
struct
{
    int i ;
    float f ;
    char ch ;
} s ;
```

(m) In C++ a structure can contain data members, as well as member functions.

Ans

True. C++ being an object-oriented language facilitates data hiding. Hence, data may not be freely accessible from outside the structure. To allow data access, functions are provided.

Q 2.27

What will be the output of the following programs:

(a)
```
#include <iostream.h>
void main( )
{
    for ( int i = 1 ; i <= 10 ; i++ )
```

```
            cout << i << endl ;
        cout << i ;
}
```

Ans

Displays 1 to 11 each in a new line.

In C++, a variable can be defined before the point of usage and not necessarily before the first executable statement. Even if the variable is defined within the parenthesis of the _for_ statement its scope is not limited to the _for_ block. But if the variable is defined inside the _for_ block (within the braces) the scope and life would be limited to that block only.

(b)
```
#include <iostream.h>
void main( )
{
    char *p = "hello" ;
    char *q = p ;
    cout << p << endl << q ;
    q = "Good Bye" ;
    cout << endl << p << endl << q ;
}
```

Ans

The output would be:

```
hello
hello
hello
Good Bye
```

Initially, both p and q contain address of the same string "hello", so "hello" gets printed twice. Then the base address of a string "Good Bye" is assigned to q. Hence, the second _cout_ statement prints "hello" and "Good Bye".

(c)   #include <iostream.h>
```
void main( )
{
    int i ;
    cout << sizeof ( i ) << endl << sizeof ( 'i' ) ;
}
```

Ans

The output would be:

2 (under DOS) or 4 (under Windows)
1

The size of an integer can be either 2 bytes or 4 bytes depending upon the operating system in use. Under DOS the size of an *int* is 2 bytes and under Windows it is 4 bytes. The size of a character constant is always 1 byte.

(d)   #include <iostream.h>
```
int i = 20 ;
void main( )
{
    int i = 5 ;
    cout << i << endl << ::i ;
    {
        int i = 10 ;
        cout << endl << i << endl << ::i ;
    }
}
```

Ans

The output would be:

5
20
10

20

In the first *cout* statement, the first *i* is being treated as the local one because it is most local in the block. The second *i* is preceded with *::* hence is treated as the global one. *::* is a scope resolution operator which resolves the scope conflict and treat variables or functions as global. In the second *cout* statement the first *i* is treated as the most local which is the one defined in the inner block. The second *i* is treated as global because the *::* operator is preceded.

(e)   #include <iostream.h>

```
void main( )
{
    int i = 5 ;
    int &j = i ;
    int p = 10 ;

    j = p ;
    cout << endl << i << endl << j ;
    p = 20 ;
    cout << endl << i << endl << j ;
}
```

Ans

The output would be:

10
10
10
10

j is a reference to *i*. This means *j* is a constant pointer to *i*. The statement *j = p* changes the value of *i* and not *j*. This is because *j* being a reference gets de-referenced automatically as (*j). Hence the value at the address stored in *j* (value of *i*) is replaced by the value of *p*.

(f)   #include <iostream.h>

```
const int  i = 10 ;
void main( )
{
    const int  i = 20 ;
    cout << i << endl << ::i ;
    cout << endl << &i << endl << &::i ;
}
```

Ans

The output would be:

```
20
10
0x0065FDF4
0x0042601C
```

The most local value of *i* gets printed first. Then with the help of scope resolution operator the value of the global variable *i* gets printed. In the second *cout*, the addresses of the local and global variables get printed out.

(g)   #include <iostream.h>

```
void main( )
{
    int  i = 15 ;
    const int  &j = i ;
    cout << i  << endl << j << endl ;
    i = 9 ;
    cout << i << endl << j ;
}
```

Ans

The output would be:

15
15
9
9

j is a constant reference. This means that using *j* we cannot change the value of *i*. But *i* being a non-constant variable its value can be changed using the statement *i = 9*.

Q 2.28

Point out the errors, if any, in the following programs:

(a) ```
#include <iostream.h>
void main( )
{
    enum result { first, second, third } ;
    result a = first ;
    int b = a ;
    result c = 1 ;
    result d = result (1) ;
}
```

### Ans

Error in the statement,

result c = 1 ;

An *int* value cannot be assigned to an *enum* variable.

(b)  ```
#include <iostream.h>
void main( )
{
```

```
int i = 5 ;
int &j = i ;
int &k = j ;
int &l = i ;

cout << i << j << k << l ;
}
```

Ans

No error. Here, same variable is tied to multiple references. The statement *int &k = j* is interpreted by the compiler as *int *const k = & *j*. Here *j* contains address of *i*. **j* gives value of *i* and then its address is taken using &. Hence address of *i* is getting stored in *k*. This again means that the reference *k* is being tied to the variable *i*.

(c)   #include <iostream.h>

```
void main( )
{
    char *p = "Hello" ;
    p = "Hi" ;
    *p = 'G' ;
    cout << p ;
}
```

Ans

The code will not give any error in Turbo.C++ for DOS but gives a runtime error in Visual C++. In Visual C++, by default "Hello" is treated as a constant string. Hence **p = 'G'* shows a runtime error because the constant string "Hello" is being changed. In Turbo C++, "Hello" is not treated as a constant string, hence can be changed.

(d)   const int a = 124 ;

```
void main( )
{
    const int *sample( ) ;
    int *p ;
    p = sample( ) ;
}

const int *sample( )
{
    return ( &a ) ;
}
```

Ans

Error in the statement $p = sample( )$. The *sample( )* function returns an address of a *const int* variable. This address is being assigned to p, which is of type *int* *. Hence a type mismatch.

(e)   #include <iostream.h>

```
void main( )
{
    char t[ ] = "String functions are simple" ;
    int l = strlen ( t ) ;
    cout << l ;
}
```

Ans

Error. The declaration of the *strlen( )* function is not available. To provide declaration of *strlen( )* function we need to include "string.h" file.

(f)   int a = 10 ;

```
void main( )
{
```

```
int  a = 20 ;
{
    int  a = 30 ;
    cout << a << ::a << ::::a ;
}
}
```

Ans

Error. There is no such operator ::::.

(g)   #include <iostream.h>

```
const int  i = 10 ;
void main( )
{
    const int  i = 20 ;
    cout << &i << &::i ;
}
```

Ans

No error.

(h)   #include <iostream.h>

```
void main( )
{
    int  a = 10, b = 20 ;
    long int  c ;
    c = a * long int ( b ) ;
    cout << c ;
}
```

Ans

No error. Both the type casts mentioned below are acceptable.

c = a * (long int) b ;

```
        c = a * long int ( b ) ;
(i)     #include <iostream.h>

        struct emp
        {
            char  name [ 20 ] ;
            int  age ;
            float  sal ;
        } ;

        emp  e1 = { "Amol", 21, 2345.00 } ;
        emp  e2 = { "Ajay", 19, 2300.00 } ;

        void main( )
        {
            emp &fun( ) ;
            fun( ) = e2 ;
            cout << endl << e1.name << endl << e1.age << endl << e1.sal ;
        }

        emp &fun( )
        {
            emp  e3 = { "Aditya", 21, 3300.75 } ;
            return e3 ;
        }
```

Ans

No error. The function call can exist on left-hand side of assignment operator. This way of calling a function can be used when a function returns a reference.

Q 2.29

In the following program how would you define *q*, if the first *cout* were to output "Internet" twice, whereas, the second *cout* is to output "Intranet" twice.

```
#include <iostream.h>

void main( )
{
    char *p = "Internet" ;
    cout << p << q ;
    q = "Intranet" ;
    cout << p << q ;
}
```

Ans

```
char* &q = p ;
```

Q 2.30

Can the following statements be written in any other way:

```
employee *p ;
p = ( employee * ) malloc ( sizeof ( e ) ) ;
float q ;
int a, b ;
q = ( float ) a / b ;
```

Ans

```
employee *p ;
p = ( employee * ) malloc ( sizeof ( e ) ) ;
float q ;
int a, b ;
q = float ( a ) / b ;
```

Q 2.31

Create four integers, four pointers to these integers and four references to them. Store these pointers and references in two arrays and print out the values of four integers using these arrays.

Ans

```
#include <iostream.h>

void main( )
{
    int a = 0, b = 1, c = 2, d = 3 ;
    int *p1 = &a, *p2 = &b, *p3 = &c, *p4 = &d ;
    int &r1 = a , &r2 = b, &r3 = c, &r4 = d ;

    // we cannot create an array of references
    int *arr[ ] = { p1, p2, p3, p4 } ;  // array of pointers

    for ( int i = 0 ; i <= 3 ; i++ )
        cout << *arr[ i ] << endl ;
}
```

Q 2.32

Complete the following program by defining the function *swapb( )* and its prototype such that the output of the program is 20 10.

```
#include <iostream.h>

void swapa ( int &, int & ) ;

void main( )
{
    int a = 10, b = 20 ;

    swapa ( a, b ) ;
    cout << a << b ;
}

void swapa ( int &x, int &y )
{
    swapb ( x, y ) ;
}
```

Ans

```
void swapb ( int &m, int &n )
{
    int t ;
    t = m ;
    m = n ;
    n = t ;
}
```

Functions

Q 3.1

What do you mean by function overloading?

Ans

Defining multiple functions with the same name is called function overloading. These functions must differ in their number, order or types of arguments.

Q 3.2

What do you mean by library functions and where are they stored?

Ans

Library functions are a collection of predefined functions. They are stored in '.lib' files that are shipped with the compiler.

Q 3.3

What are header files and what do they contain?

Ans

Header files merely contain function declarations. Header files generally have '.h' extension.

Q 3.4

Can we make our own function library and a header file?

Ans

Yes. Different compilers provide different utilities to add/delete/modify functions in the standard library. For example, Turbo C/C++ compilers provide a utility called "tlib.exe". Using this utility we can also create a completely new library. The steps given below help us to create our own function library:

(a) Write function definition in "mylib.cpp" file.

(b) Compile the "mylib.cpp" file. The "mylib.obj" file would get created.

(c) Add the function to the library by issuing the command

C:\>tlib mylib +c:\mylib.obj

Here, "mylib" is a library filename, + is a switch, which means we want to add new function to library and "c:\mylib.obj" is the path of the ".obj" file.

(d) We have to declare the function in the header file. The header file would contain only function declaration and should be included while calling the function.

(e) To use the function present inside the library, create a program, include the header file containing the function declaration and call the function. Compile the program as shown below:

C:\tc\bin> tcc –Ic:\tc\include –Lc:\tc\lib, c:\mylib.lib use.cpp

This command will create a ".exe" file. The switch –I specifies the path of the header files that might be included in the program. The path given here is "c:\tc\include". The switch –L specifies the path of the library files that might contain the functions called from the program. Since our file is stored in the root directory of drive C we have specified the complete path and the filename. Lastly, "use.cpp" is the file that contains the source code from which the library function present in "mylib" is being called.

(f) Execute the program "use.exe" from command prompt.

C:\>use.exe.

Q 3.5

In how many ways can we pass variables to a function?

Ans

There are three ways in which we can pass variables to a function:

(a) By Value

```
void fun ( int , int ) ;   // declaration
fun ( a, b ) ;  // call
```

(b) By Reference

```
void fun ( int&, int& ) ; // declaration
fun ( a, b ) ; // call
```

(c) By Address

```
void fun ( int*, int* ) ; // declaration
fun ( &a, &b ) ; // call
```

Q 3.6

What are the advantages of passing function arguments by reference or pointers over passing by value?

Ans

The main advantage of passing variables by reference or pointer is that they avoid creation of a new variable. When a large structure variable is passed by value; a new structure variable of the same size gets created in the function. This consumes memory. If the same structure variable is passed by reference or pointer, the new variable that gets created in the function would either be a reference or a pointer variable occupying only 2 or 4 bytes in memory. The second advantage is that we are able to modify the actual variable from the called function.

Q 3.7

Is it safe to return a reference of a *static* variable from a function?

Ans

Yes. A *static* variable persists across function calls. This means it remains alive even if the control returns from the called function.

Hence it is safe to return a reference of a *static* variable from a function.

Q 3.8

In a function declaration there is no need to give variable names. Still it is recommended. Why?

Ans

This is explained with the help of the following example:

The *setcur( )* function accepts two parameters: row number and column number. Hence can be declared as follows:

void setcur (int, int) ;

or

void setcur (int row, int col) ;

From the first declaration it is not clear whether row is to be passed as the first parameter or the column. But from the second declaration it is clear that we have to pass first the row number and then the column number.

Q 3.9

What is an inline function?

Ans

The function, whose code gets inserted, instead of a jump to the function, at the place where there is a function call is known an *inline* function. By making the function *inline* we request the compiler to insert the code at the place where there is a function call, so that, time is saved in calling the function and returning from the function. The compiler takes the decision whether to insert the code or not depending upon the size of the code and optimization settings of the compiler. In situations where a small function is getting called several times we can save the overhead involved in calling the function by making the function *inline*.

Q 3.10

What is the advantage of an inline function over a macro?

Ans

In case of an *inline* function the compiler takes the decision whether to insert the code or not depending upon the size of code and the compiler's optimization settings. Hence there is more likelihood of more optimized code getting generated. In case of macro, the macro expansion gets inserted irrespective of the size of code and optimization settings of the compiler.

Also, an *inline* function provides better type checking and does not have side effects typically associated with macros. For example:

```
#include <iostream.h>
#define SQUARE(x)  x * x

inline float square ( float  y )
{
    return y * y ;
}

void main( )
{
    float  a = 0.5, b = 0.5, c, d ;
```

```
    c = SQUARE ( ++a ) ;
    d = square ( ++d ) ;
}
```

During preprocessing the macro SQUARE gets expanded into

```
c = ++x * ++x ;
```

We can notice the undesirable side effect in this macro expansion. The variable is getting incremented twice even though we have used the incrementation operator only once. Such side effects would not occur in an *inline* function.

Q 3.11

How can we prevent a reference from modifying the value of a variable when the variable is passed by reference?

Ans

By making the reference *const* we can prevent it from changing the value of the variable to which it is referring.

Q 3.12

Why function overloading does not depend upon the return type?

Ans

Let us understand this with the help of an example:

```
int f( )
{
    return 9 ;
}
```

```
void f( )
{
}

void main( )
{
    f( );
}
```

There is an ambiguity in the function call. This is because just by seeing the call we cannot figure out which version of *f( )* should get called (the version that returns a value or the version that does not return a value).

Even if we are not collecting the value, we cannot assume that the function *f( )* that does not return a value would get called. This is because it is not necessary to collect the returned value even if the called function returns a value.

Q 3.13

How C++ manages function overloading?

Ans

Simple functions (non-virtual functions) are always called by their names. Since the overloaded function has same name it would become impossible to call different versions of the same function. Hence C++ compiler changes name of all the function definitions and calls while compiling the program. This is known as name mangling.

Q 3.14

What is name mangling?

Ans

Name mangling means different names are given to the different versions of an overloaded function. This is shown in the following example:

```
void f ( int i )
{
}

void f ( float f )
{
}

void f ( int i, float f )
{
}

void main( )
{
    f ( 10 ) ;
    f ( 3.5f ) ;
    f ( 10, 3.5f ) ;
}
```

The compiler changes the names of the overloaded function as follows:

Original Function Name	Mangled Function Name
void f (int i)	?f@@YAXH@Z (int i)
void f (float f)	?f@@YAXM@Z (float f)
void f (int i, float f)	?f@@YAXHM@Z (int i, float f)

The first version of the function *f( )* accepts an *int*, hence the mangled name contains *H* in it.

The second version of the function *f( )* accepts *float*, hence the mangled name contains *M* in it.

The third version of the function *f( )* accepts an *int* and *float*, hence the mangled name contains *HM* in it.

Name mangling is also known as name decoration.

Name mangling is compiler dependent. Different compiler may mangle the same function name differently. Compiler mangles the name as per the type, order and number of arguments.

Q 3.15

What is the advantage of function overloading?

Ans

Consider the following functions that return the absolute value of an argument:

```
int abs ( int i ) ;
long labs ( long l ) ;
double fabs ( double d ) ;
```

All these functions perform same job. So it is improper to have three different function names. C++ allows function overloading wherein the programmer can create three different functions with the same name but different types of arguments as shown below:

```
int abs ( int  i ) ;
long abs ( long  l ) ;
double abs ( double  d ) ;
```

With function overloading we are relieved· from remembering different function names just because their arguments are different.

Q 3.16

Where can an ambiguity occur in overloading a function?

Ans

Let's take an example:

```
void f ( int  i )
{
}

void f ( int  &i )
{
}
```

The function *f( )* is overloaded to accept an *int* value and an *int* reference. But if we call *f( )* as shown below

```
int  i = 9 ;
f ( i ) ;
```

the compiler cannot figure out whether to call the version of *f( )* that accepts a value or the one that accepts a reference. Since the syntax of calling both versions is same, it results in an ambiguity.

Q 3.17

Why C++ does not provide a way to leave the leading or middle arguments as defaults?

Ans

There could have been a way to leave the leading or middle arguments as defaults by making a call

f(, , 10, , 20);

By leaving the arguments and giving commas we could have specified which argument we intend to leave. This however poses a problem for a function that takes a large number of arguments. Imagine a situation where a function takes 20 arguments. If we want to pass the last 5 arguments we would have to provide 15 commas. There is a chance that we may give incorrect number of commas. So instead of passing last five parameters we may end up passing some other parameters.

Q 3.18

Do default values take part in mangling the names?

Ans

No.

Q 3.19

Can we give a default return value?

Ans

No.

Q 3.20

What is operator overloading?

Ans

Operator overloading means giving capability to the operator to work on different types of operands. The operators +, *, etc. work on operands of type *int*, *float*, etc. We can overload these operators by giving them the capability to work on user-defined data types.

For example, to add two structure variables of type *data* we can write the following code:

```
struct data
{
    int i;
    float f;
};

data c, a = { 1, 2.5f }, b = { 3, 5.5f };

c = a + b;
```

instead of,

```
c.i = a.i + b.i;
c.f = a.f + b.f;
```

In $a + b$, the '+' operator is overloaded to add two structure variables. We would of course have to provide the overloaded *operator +* function to carry out the addition.

Q 3.21

Can we change the precedence of operators using operator overloading?

Ans

No.

Q 3.22

What are the advantages of operator overloading?

Ans

By making the operators to work on user defined data types just like they work on built-in data types, we can have a consistent approach.

Also, it is more intuitive to overload an operator rather than calling a function to perform the same job. This provides clarity to the program. For example, if *a* and *b* are variables of some user-defined data type, then writing $a + b$ is more intuitive than calling a function *add (a, b)*.

The situation becomes more impractical when *a*, *b*, *c* and *d* are to be added. Using the function we can achieve this through

add (d, add (c, add (a, b))) ;

But using the '+' operator the addition can be performed as $a + b + c + d$. This is known as cascading the operator. Even different operators can be cascaded like $a + b - c * d / e$.

Q 3.23

How does the cascading of operators' work?

Ans

Let's take an example:

```cpp
struct data
{
    int i ;
    float f ;
} ;

data operator + ( data x, data y )
{
    // code
}

data operator * ( data x, data y )
{
    // code
}

data operator - ( data x, data y )
{
    // code
}

data operator / ( data x, data y )
{
    // code
}

void main( )
{
    data a = { 1, 2.5f }, b = { 2, 3.5f }, c = { 3, 4.5f }, d = { 4, 5.5f }, e = { 5, 6.5f };
    data s ;
```

```
s = a + b * c / d - e;
}
```

In this program *a, b, c, d, e* and *s* are user-defined data types. The operators '+', '*', '–', '/' and '=' are overloaded to work on these user-defined data types. The statement is executed as per the precedence of operators. Hence *b * c* would be performed first. This operation gets expanded to *operator * (b, c)*. The corresponding function definition gets called. The multiplication is performed and the result is returned. The resultant statement would become *a + result / d – e*. Now division would be performed by calling the function *operator / ( )* with the *result of addition* and *d* as the parameters. Likewise, other operations would be performed and the result would be assigned to *s* using the overloaded *operator = ( )* function. Since the overloaded *operator = ( )* function is provided by the compiler we are not required to define it.

Q 3.24

Can you point out a situation where a reference becomes indispensable?

Ans

When we want to save memory while collecting arguments of a large structure type in the overloaded operator functions, pointers cannot be used. For example, if the + operator is overloaded and we use an expression *a + b*. If *b* is a big structure then while passing it to the overloaded operator + function if we wish to prevent a copy of *b* from getting created then we cannot pass *b* as a pointer. We have to pass it by reference.

Q 3.25

While overloading a binary operator can we provide default values?

Ans

No. This is because even if we provide the default arguments to the parameters of the overloaded operator function we would end up using the binary operator incorrectly. This is explained in the following example:

```
data operator + ( data  x, data  y = { 2, 3.5f } )
{
}

void main( )
{
    data  s, a, b ;
    s = a + ;  // error
}
```

Q 3.26

Write function prototypes for the following:

(a)   A function which receives an *int* and a *float* and returns a *double*.

Ans

```
double fun ( int, float ) ;
```

(b)   A function that receives an *int* pointer and *float* reference and returns an *int* pointer.

Ans

int* fun (int*, float&) ;

(c) A function which doesn't receive anything and doesn't return anything.

Ans

void fun (void) ;
or

void fun1( ) ;

(d) A function that receives an array of *int*s, and a *float* reference and doesn't return anything.

Ans

void fun (int [ ], float&) ;
or

void fun1(int*, float&) ;

Q 3.27

How can we differentiate between a pre and post increment operator while overloading?

Ans

Mentioning the keyword *int* as the second parameter in the post increment form of the *operator++( )* helps distinguish between the two forms. This is shown in the following example:

#include <iostream.h>

```
struct data
{
    int i ;
} ;

data operator++ ( data  x ) // pre-increment
{
    data t ;
    x.i = x.i + 1 ;
    t.i = x.i ;
    return t ;
}

data operator++ ( data x, int ) // post-increment
{
    data t ;
    t.i = x.i ;
    x.i = x.i + 1 ;
    return t ;
}

void main( )
{
    data  a = { 2 }, s ;
    s = a++ ;
    s = ++a ;
}
```

Q 3.28

Do the function call and definition both get mangled?

Ans

Yes. ·

Q 3.29

Do all functions in C++ get mangled?

Ans

Yes. The C++ compiler mangles all the functions irrespective of whether the function has been overloaded or not.

Q 3.30

How name mangling can be prevented?

Ans

To avoid name mangling the function should be declared with *extern "C"* attribute. Functions declared as *extern "C"* are treated as C-style functions. Hence the compiler does not mangle them. This is shown below:

```
#include <iostream.h>

extern "C" void display( )
{
    cout << "See the effect of C in C++ " ;
}

void main( )
{
    display( ) ;
}
```

Q 3.31

State whether the following statements are True or False:

(a) Constants are always passed by value to a function.

> **Ans**
>
> False. We can pass constants by reference also. But while receiving the parameters in function we have to receive it in a variable declared as *const*. This is shown in the following example:
>
> ```
> #include <iostream.h>
>
> void fun ( const int& i )
> {
>     cout << i ;
> }
>
> void main( )
> {
>         fun ( 7 );
> }
> ```
>
> It is necessary to specify a reference as *const*. If we do not do so then using the reference we may try to modify 7. This is not possible as 7 is a constant.

(b) A function can be overloaded if the arguments are similar but the return values are different.

Ans

False. Function overloading is allowed only when functions having the same name differ in number, order or type of arguments.

(c) If default values are mentioned for the four arguments in the function prototype, we can call this function and pass it the first and the fourth argument.

Ans

False. The default arguments can only be trailing arguments. This means that we can leave only the trailing arguments while calling the function so that the default arguments can get used. C++ provides no way to leave leading or middle arguments as default arguments while calling the function.

(d) A function can be overloaded any number of times.

Ans

True.

(e) The assignment operator cannot be overloaded.

Ans

False. We are never required to provide an overloaded assignment operator because the compiler provides one by default. The default assignment operator just copies the value of right-hand side variable into the left-hand side variable.

(f)   When we define the function to be inline there is no guarantee that its code would get inserted at the place where the call is being made.

Ans

True. The inline function may work as a macro or simply as a function. This wholly depends upon the compiler. If the function contains lot of code and the compiler is set to optimize the code in terms of memory requirement then the function call would not be replaced by its code. If the compiler is set to optimize the code in terms of speed then the function call might get replaced by its code. Hence by declaring inline we are just making a request to the compiler. C++ language does not define under what conditions the compiler may choose to ignore our request. Hence compiler writers have the flexibility in how they interpret the requirements.

(g)   The ++ operator can be overloaded to perform decrementation of a variable.

Ans

True. To overload any operator we have to define a function. There is no restriction on what goes inside that function. But it is not recommended to change the actual meaning of any operator. Moral – don't overload the ++ *operator* to perform a -- job.

(h)   All operators available in C++ can be overloaded.

Ans

False. The operators that cannot be overloaded are shown below.

Operator	Known as
.	Member selection
.*	Pointer-to-member selection
::	Scope resolution
? :	Conditional

The operators "." and ".*" are means of referring structure or class members. They take name rather than a value as their second operand. For example, when we say *p.a*, *a* is a name rather than a value. *p.a* is the value. Since to an overloaded operator function we must pass a value and not the name we are not allowed to overload the "." operator.

The "::" operator refers to a variable rather than a value. Hence it cannot be overloaded.

Even though ? : are operators they do not perform an operation as such. They offer a compact way of representing a simple *if-else*. Hence they cannot be overloaded.

(i)   While overloading a binary operator if we want to prevent making a copy of the variables that are passed as arguments, a pointer can be used to collect the parameters.

Ans

False. Consider the statement $c = a + b$ where the + operator has been overloaded.

This statement would be interpreted by the compiler as $c = operator + (a, b)$. Since here addresses of variables are not getting passed we cannot collect them in pointer variables. If we want to collect them in pointer variables we have to modify the statement as follows:

c = &a + &b ;

But this means that we are trying to add addresses of a & b and not their values. At such times only references can be used to save memory.

Q 3.32

Point out the errors, if any, in the following programs:

(a)   void f (int x, int y) ;

```
void main( )
{
    f( ) ;
}

void f ( int x = 0, int y = 0 )
{
    cout << x << endl << y ;
}
```

Ans

Error. In this program the declaration is used to analyze the function call since the declaration occurs before the function call. Hence it is necessary to specify default arguments in the declaration and not in the definition. If the definition is placed before the function call then default arguments can be specified in the definition. If both declaration as well as definition occur before the function call then we can specify default arguments in any of them. Basically it means that compiler must know the default values before the call is encountered.

(b)   void main( )
       {
           int a = 30 ;
           f( ) ;
       }

       void f( )
       {
           int b = 20 ;
       }

   Ans

   Error. In C++, before calling a function, its prototype must be mentioned. If not, then the function must be defined before calling it. This is because the compiler compiles the program from top to bottom. While compiling the compiler uses the signature (name, number of arguments, argument types and order of arguments) of the function to build the call. When a function call is encountered before its prototype or the definition the signature of the function is not known to the compiler and hence it flashes an error.

(c)   #include <iostream.h>
       void f( )
       {
           cout << "Hello" ;
       }

```
void main( )
{
    f( ) ;
}
```

Ans

No Error. When function definition occurs before the call then there is no need to mention its prototype. This is because the function definition contains all the necessary information that is needed by the compiler to build the call. Refer (b) above for details.

(d)   `#include <iostream.h>`

```
int f ( int, int ) ;
int f ( int, int ) ;

void main( )
{
    int  a ;
    a = f ( 10, 30 ) ;
    cout << a ;
}

void f ( int  x, int  y )
{
    return x + y ;
}
```

Ans

Error. Function definition should match with the function declaration. Here, when the function *f( )* is declared its return type is mentioned as *int* whereas when it is defined the return type is *void*.

(e) ```
     #include <iostream.h>
     void main( )
     {
         void f (void) ;
         void g (void) ;
         f( ) ;
     }

     void f (void)
     {
         g( ) ;
         cout << endl << "Hi...Hello" ;
     }

     void g (void)
     {
         cout << endl << "to you" ;
     }
     ```

### Ans

Error. The compiler flashes an error in the line where *g( )* is being called. This is because the declaration of *g( )* is not available in the function *f( )* since the declaration is local in *main( )*.

Thus, declaration of a function should be mentioned in the function from where the call is materializing. A better way is to declare the function as global so that its declaration becomes available to all the functions in the program.
     ```

(f)   #include <iostream.h>

```
void f ( int = 10, int = 20, int = 30 ) ;
void f ( int, int ) ;

void main( )
{
    f ( 1, 2 ) ;
}

void f ( int x, int y, int z )
{
    cout << endl << x << endl << y << endl << z ;
}

void f ( int x, int y )
{
    cout << endl << x << endl << y ;
}
```

Ans

Error. There is an ambiguity in the function call. This is because one version of *f( )* accepts two parameters and the other version can accept either 0, 1, 2 or 3 parameters since we have given all the parameters a default value. When *f( )* is called with two parameters, compiler fails to decide which version of *f( )* to call.

Q 3.33

Write overloaded functions to convert an *int* to an ascii string and to convert a *float* to an ascii string.

Ans

```
#include <iostream.h>
#include <stdio.h>
#include <stdlib.h>

void toascii ( float f, char *s )
{
    sprintf ( s, "%f", f ) ;
}

void toascii ( int i, char *s )
{
    itoa ( i, s, 10 ) ;
}

void main( )
{
    float f = 9.342f ;
    int i = 73 ;

    char fstr [ 20 ] ;
    char istr [ 20 ] ;

    toascii ( f, fstr ) ;
    toascii ( i, istr ) ;
    cout << fstr << endl ;
    cout << istr ;
}
```

Q 3.34

Write overloaded functions to convert an ascii string to an *int* and to convert an ascii string to a *float*.

Ans

```
#include <iostream.h>
#include <stdio.h>
#include <stdlib.h>

void fromascii ( float *f, char *s )
{
    sscanf ( s, "%f", f ) ;
}

void fromascii ( int *i, char *s )
{
    *i = atoi ( s ) ;
}

void main( )
{
    float f ;
    int i ;

    char  fstr[ ] = "7.897" ;
    char  istr[ ] = "73" ;

    fromascii ( &f, fstr ) ;
    fromascii ( &i, istr ) ;

    cout << f << endl ;
    cout << i ;
}
```

Classes in C++

Q 4.1

What are the two major components of an object?

Ans

Data members and the member functions that operate upon the data are the major components of an object.

Q 4.2

Point out the reasons why using *new* is a better idea than using *malloc( )?*

Ans

Since *malloc( )* returns a *void* pointer it is necessary to explicitly typecast it into an appropriate type of pointer. This gets completely avoided when we are using the *new operator*. For example:

```
int  * p1 = ( int * ) malloc ( sizeof ( int ) ) ;
float  * p2 = ( float * ) malloc ( sizeof ( float )  ) ;
sample  * p3 = ( sample * ) malloc ( sizeof ( sample ) ) ;
```

Here, *sample* is a user-defined class.

```
int * p1 = new int ;
int * p2 = new int [ 30 ] ;
sample * p3 = new sample ;
```

Another difference between *new* and *malloc( )* is that *new* automatically calls the constructor while *malloc( )* doesn't. Also, *new* being an operator, it can be overloaded.

Q 4.3

Design a class from which we can create objects by passing one, two or three arguments. The *class* should not have more than one constructor function.

Ans

```
class threeinone
{
    int i, j, k ;

    public :

        threeinone ( int ii = 0, int jj = 0, int kk = 0 )
        {
            i = ii ;
            j = jj ;
            k = kk ;
        }
} ;

void main( )
{
    threeinone  one ( 1 ) ;
    threeinone  two ( 1, 2 ) ;
    threeinone  three ( 1, 2, 3 ) ;
}
```

Q 4.4

What is the difference between the following two statements if *a* is a pointer to an array allocated dynamically?

delete a ;
delete [ ] a ;

Ans

The statement, *delete a*, deletes the complete array. But if the array is an array of objects, then the destructor would be called only for the first object in the array. The statement, *delete[ ] a*, deletes the complete array and calls the destructor for each object in the array.

Q 4.5

What does the *delete* operator do in addition to deallocating the memory used by the object?

Ans

delete calls the destructor of the class whose object is being destroyed.

Q 4.6

How many access specifiers are there in C++?

Ans

There are three access specifiers in C++: *public, protected* and *private. public* data members or member functions can be accessed from anywhere, within the *class* or from outside the *class. private* data members cannot be accessed from outside the *class*. They can only be accessed within the *class*. The *protected* access specifier would be discussed in Chapter 7.

Q 4.7

Can we define member functions outside the *class*?

Ans

Refer Q 4.49 (r).

Q 4.8

How can we call member functions from outside the *class*?

Ans

To call any non-static member function, we always need to have an object of that class. To call a static member function, either an object or the class can be used.

Q 4.9

Can we access *private* data members from the outside the *class*?

Ans

No. *private* data members are only accessible from within the *class*.

There is a way in which you can access or change the *private* data of a *class* but doing so violates the object-oriented programming concepts. Following code would help you out as to how to access the private data members.

```
#include <iostream.h>

class sample
{
    private :

        int i ;

    public :

        sample ( int ii )
        {
```

```
                i = ii ;
        }

        void display( )
        {
             cout << i << endl ;
        }
} ;

void main( )
{
     sample  s ( 97 ) ;
     s.display( ) ;
     int * p = ( int * ) &s ;
     *p = 43 ;
     s.display( ) ;
}
```

In the above example we are storing the address of the object *s* in the pointer *p*. Ideally *p* should be of the type *sample**, but we have defined it to be of type *int**. So while storing the address of object *s* we have to explicitly typecast it. After storing the address of the object *s* we can easily access the data at that address which is noting but the *private* data.

Q 4.10

How can we initialize an array of objects?

Ans

This is explained with the help of an example:

```
#include <iostream.h>

class sample
{
     int i ;
```

```
        float f ;

        public :

            sample ( int  ii, float  ff )
            {
                    i = ii ;
                    f = ff ;
            }
};

void main( )
{
    sample  p [ 5 ] = {
                        sample ( 1, 2.5f ),
                        sample ( 3, 4.5f ),
                        sample ( 12, 0.0f ),
                        sample ( 32, 6.4f ),
                        sample ( 23, 14.7f )
                    } ;
}
```

Here, *p* is an array of *sample* objects. To initialize the array we are required to create those many objects and assign their values to the elements of the array.

Q 4.11

Why data members of the class or structure cannot be initialized at the point of declaration?

Ans

Whenever we declare a class or a structure no memory is allocated, hence there is no question of storing data in data members. The memory is allocated for data members only when an object of the class or variable of structure is created.

Q 4.12

How can we initialize a *const* data member?

Ans

The *const* data member should be initialized as shown below:

```
class sample
{
     const int  i ;

     public :

          sample( ) : i ( 3 )
          {
          }
};
```

Q 4.13

In the following code, what change would you make to initialize the value of *i* to 10?

```
class sample
{
     int i ;

     public :

          sample ( int  ii )
          {
               i = ii ;
          }
};

class comp
{
     private :
```

```
            sample s ;

        public :

            comp ( int ii )
            {
            }
};

void main( )
{
    comp c ( 10 );
}
```

Ans

The following change should be made in the constructor.
```
comp ( int ii ) : s ( ii )
{
}
```

Q 4.14

Do member functions occupy space in objects?

Ans

Refer Q 4.49 (m)

Q 4.15

What is an anonymous *class*?

Ans

Whenever a *class* is defined without any name (tag) then that *class* is said to be an anonymous *class*. For example:

```
class
{
    int i ;
    float f ;
} obj ;
```

obj is an object of the anonymous *class*. Anonymous *class*es are typically used with *typedef* to create a convenient name as shown below:

```
typedef class
{
    int a ;
    float b
    char ch ;
} sample ;
sample s ;
```

Q 4.16

How would you *typedef* a *class* to some simple name?

Ans

Following program shows this:

```
typedef class sample
{
    int i ;
    float f ;
} petname ;
```

Here, *petname* is another name given to *class sample*.

Q 4.17

Can we assign one object to another object of the same type through = operator?

Ans

Yes. By default the compiler provides an overloaded assignment operator to the user-defined classes and structures to carry out this assignment.

Q 4.18

Which function gets called when we assign an object of a *class* to another object of the same type?

Ans

Whenever an object is assigned to another object of the same type, an overloaded assignment operator gets called.

Q 4.19

What change would you make in the following class if *c.display( )* is to output 10 12.04?

```cpp
#include <iostream.h>

class sample
{
    private :

        int i ;
        float f ;

    public :

        sample ( int ii = 0, float ff = 0.0f )
        {
            i = ii ;
            f = ff ;
        }

        void display( )
        {
```

```
                    cout << i << endl << f ;
            }
};

void main( )
{
    sample  a ( 3, 2.9f ), b ( 7, 9.14f ), c ;
    c = a + b ;
    c.display( ) ;
}
```

Ans

We need to overload the + operator as shown below:

```
sample operator + ( sample  s )
{
    sample  t ;
    t.i = i + s.i ;
    t.f = f + s.f ;
    return  t ;
}
```

Q 4.20

Can we initiate an object *s* of class *sample* through a statement,

```
sample  s = 10 ;
```

Ans

Compiler will treat the statement as *sample s (10)*. If there is a one-argument constructor within the class *sample*, the statement would work but if there is no one-argument constructor then the compiler will flash an error.

Q 4.21

Can we initiate an object *s* of class *sample* through a statement, sample s = 10, 20 ;

Ans

The compiler would flash an error, as this syntax cannot call a two-argument constructor.

Q 4.22

What is the difference between the following statements?

sample s1( ) ;
sample s2 (10, 20) ;

Ans

It appears that in the first statement we are creating an object *s1* using a zero-argument constructor. However, in actuality the statement is treated as the prototype of function *s1( )* whose return type is *sample*. To create an object using a zero-argument constructor the statement we should use is:

sample s1 ;

In the second statement an object is created using the two-argument constructor.

Q 4.23

What is a memory leak?

Ans

When we allocate memory dynamically but somehow lose the way to reach that memory then it is called as memory leak.

For example, suppose there is a function wherein we allocate memory dynamically and store its address in a pointer that is local to that function. When the control returns from the function, the local pointer dies losing the address of the memory it was pointing to. The dynamically allocated memory would continue to remain allocated, yet inaccessible. This allocated memory is leaked memory since we have lost the way to access it. This is shown in the following example:

```
void fun( )
{
    int *p = new int ;
    // code
}

void main( )
{
    fun( ) ;
    // code
}
```

When control returns from the function memory gets leaked.

Q 4.24

What is a dangling pointer?

Ans

Suppose we allocate a chunk of memory and store its address in a pointer. If this chunk of memory is freed and if the pointer continues to point to that location, the pointer is said to be a dangling pointer. For example:

```
#include <iostream.h>

void main( )
{
    int *p ;
    int *q = new int ;
    p = q ;
    delete q ;
    // code
}
```

In this example *p* and *q* are pointing to the same location in memory. The statement *delete q* would free the allocated memory making *p* a dangling pointer.

Q 4.25

What is the size of an object of an empty class? And Why?

Ans

The size of an object of an empty class is one byte. Since C++ allows us to create the object of an empty class it should have some bytes of memory. The minimum amount of memory that could be reserved is 1 byte. Hence the object size turns out to be 1 byte.

Q 4.26

How a member function comes to know on which object it has to work upon?

Ans

Whenever a member function gets called an address of the object that calls it gets passed to the function. This address gets collected in the *this* pointer through which the function can understand on which object it has to work on. Refer Q 4.49 (o).

Q 4.27

What is the type of *this* pointer?

Ans

If *sample* is the name of the *class* whose function is called through its object, then the type of *this* pointer would be,

sample *const this

Q 4.28

When does a *this* pointer get created?

Ans

The *this* pointer gets created when a member function (non-static) of a *class* is called.

Q 4.29

If a member function has formal parameters with the same name as the data members of the *class* as shown below:

```
class sample
{
    int i ;
    float f ;

    public :

        void setdata ( int i, float f )
        {
            i = i ;
            f = f ;
        }
};
```

then which variables would be given the priority inside the function? How would we distinguish between them?

Ans

It is always the formal parameters, which would get the priority. Writing '*this* ->' before the variables which we want to treat as data members of the *class* distinguishes them from the formal parameters. For example,

```
class sample
```

```
{
    prvate :

        int i ;
        float f ;

    public :

        void setdata ( int i, float f )
        {
            this -> i = i ;
            this -> f = f ;
        }
};
```

Here, *this -> i* and *this -> f* both refer to the data members of the class *sample*. The variables *i* and *f* that are on the right hand side of the assignment operator are treated as formal arguments of the function *setdata( )*.

Q 4.30

Can member functions of a *class* access global data or global functions?

Ans

Yes. The way to access global data and global functions is to use the scope resolution operator (::). This is shown in the following example:

```
int i = 9 ;

void f( )
{
}

class sample
```

```
{
    public :

        void create( )
        {
            int  x = ::i ;
            ::f( ) ;
        }
};
```

Q 4.31

What happens when we call a constructor explicitly?

Ans

Whenever the constructor is called explicitly a nameless object gets created. For example,

```
class sample
{
    int  i ;

    public :

        sample ( int  i = 0 )
        {
        }
};

void main( )
{
    sample s ; // implicit call
    s = sample ( 3 ) ; // explicit call
}
```

At the time of creation of the object *s* the constructor gets called automatically (implicitly). When the statement *s = sample (3)* is executed the constructor is called explicitly and a nameless object gets created whose value gets assigned to *s*.

Q 4.32

Can we create an object dynamically?

Ans

Yes. The keyword *new* allows us to create an object dynamically. This is shown in the following code snippet:

```
sample *p = new sample ;
```

Assume that *sample* is a user-defined *class*. *new sample* creates an object dynamically and the address of that object is returned which has been collected in *p*.

Q 4.33

How can we call member functions through a pointer to an object?

Ans

To call the member functions through a pointer to an object we have to use the arrow operator (->). For example:

```
sample *s = new sample ;
s -> fun( ) ;
```

Here, *s* is a pointer to an object of the class *sample* and *fun( )* is the member function of the *sample* class.

Q 4.34

How would you create a two-argument object dynamically?

Ans

This can be explained with the help of following example:

```
class sample
{
```

```
    int i ;

    public :

        sample ( int ii, float ff )
        {
            // code
        }
} ;

void main( )
{
    sample *p = new sample ( 62, 78.31f ) ;
}
```

The same cannot be done if *malloc( )* is used instead of the *new.*

Q 4.35

Can a destructor be called explicitly to delete an object?

Ans

No. This is because destructor gets called when an object is about to get destroyed. Hence calling it explicitly doesn't serve any purpose.

Q 4.36

Does the *delete* operator call the destructor of the *class*?

Ans

Yes. Just before deallocating the memory the delete operator calls the destructor of the class. The same does not happen if *free( )* is used in place of *delete.* The *free( )* function only deallocates memory but does not call the destructor.

Q 4.37

What do we mean by binary operators?

Ans

Operators that work on two operands are called binary operators. For example, +, -, *, %, etc.

Q 4.38

Can we overload pre-increment ++ and post-increment ++ operators? How?

Ans

Yes. By defining the *operator ++ ( )* function in the *class* we can overload pre-increment ++ *operator*. For overloading post-increment ++ *operator* we have to define *operator ++ (int)* function. To differentiate between the pre and post-increment ++ operators, the *int* is used in the post-increment ++ operator function. Following example shows the difference between the post-increment and pre-increment operators.

```
class sample
{
        // code

    public :

        sample operator ++ ( )  // pre-increment
        {
            // code
        }

        sample operator ++ ( int ) // post-increment
        {
            // code
        }
```

};

Note that if the post-increment ++ operator is not defined then for both ++c and c++ the pre-increment ++ operator function gets called. Vice-versa is however not true.

Q 4.39

What happens when we add an *int* value to a user-defined type of object?

Ans

```
class sample
{
    private :

        int i ;
        float f ;

    public :

        sample ( int ii = 0, float ff = 0.0f )
        {
            i = ii ;
            f = ff ;
        }

        sample operator + ( sample  s )
        {
            sample  t ;
            t.i = i + s.i ;
            t.f = f + s.f ;
            return  t ;
        }
};

void main( )
```

```
{
    sample  s1 ( 3, 7.2f ), s2 ;
    s2 = s1 + 10 ;
    s2 = 20 + s1 ; // error
}
```

In this example the statement *s2 = s1 + 10* gets converted to *s2 = s1.operator + (10)*. Since *s1* is an object of the *sample* class the *operator + ( )* of the *sample* class gets called. The value 10 gets passed to it which gets collected in *s*, hence it becomes sample *s = 10*. Here *s* is getting created and at the same time it is being initialized, hence a one-argument constructor gets called. Since the *sample* class has a one-argument constructor, *s* gets initialized and the overloaded + operator works fine.

But the statement *s2 = 20 + s1* gets expanded to *s2 = 20.operator + (s1)*. 20 being an *int* this would call the *operator + ( )* function of the *int* class. Since there is no such function in the *int* class it would search for a conversion operator in the *int* class that can convert an *int* to a *sample* object. Again there is no conversion operator, hence it results in an error. This error can be avoided by providing a *friend* function, which is discussed in detail in Chapter 10.

Q 4.40

In the following code if *cout << i* is to output 3 then what change should you make in the class *sample*?

```
#include <iostream.h>

class sample
{
    int i ;
    float f ;

    public :
```

```
            sample ( int ii, float ff )
            {
                    i = ii ;
                    f = ff ;
            }
};

void main( )
{
        sample  s ( 3, 7.2f ) ;
        int  i = s ;
        cout << i ;
}
```

Ans

To convert an object of type *sample* into an integer we need to provide a conversion operator function in the class *sample* as shown below:

```
operator int( )  // conversion operator
{
        return this -> i ;
}
```

Q 4.41

How to overload the following binary operators +, +=, <=, >=, !=, ==.

Ans

```
#include <iostream.h>

class sample
{
        int i ;
```

```cpp
public :

    sample ( int  ii )
    {
        i = ii ;
    }

    sample operator + ( sample  s )
    {
        return sample ( i + s.i ) ;
    }

    sample operator += ( sample  s )
    {
        return sample ( i += s.i ) ;
    }

    bool operator <= ( sample  s )
    {
        if ( i <= s.i )
            return true ;
        else
            return false ;
    }

    bool operator >= ( sample  s )
    {
        if ( i >= s.i )
            return true ;
        else
            return false ;
    }

    bool operator != ( sample  s )
    {
        if ( i != s.i )
            return true ;
        else
```

```
                        return false ;
                }

                bool operator == ( sample  s )
                {
                        if ( i == s.i )
                                return true ;
                        else
                                return false ;
                }
};

void main( )
{
        sample  a ( 1 ), b ( 2 ), c ( 0 ) ;
        c = a + b ;
        if ( a <= b )
                cout << "a is less than or equal to b" << endl ;
        a += b ;
        if ( a >= b )
                cout << "a is greater than or equal to b " << endl ;
        if ( a != b )
                cout << "a and b are not equal" << endl ;
        if ( a == c )
                cout << "a and c are equal" << endl ;
}
```

Q 4.42

How would the following statement be expanded?

s = a + b + c + d ;

Ans

Firstly, the *operator + ( )* function would get called using *a* and to it *b* would get passed. Thus the call becomes *a.operator + (b)*, and the statement becomes, s = (a.operator + (b)) + c + d ;

After adding *a* and *b* their result is returned as an object and then using this object the *opearator + ( )* function is called and *c* is passed as a parameter. Thus the call becomes *result.operator + (c)*. And the code becomes,

s = (result.operator + (c)) + d ;

This again returns a result after adding *c*, which then calls *operator + ( )* function by passing *i*. Hence the code becomes,

s = result.operator + (d) ;

This returns the final result that is then assigned to *s*.

Q 4.43

Implement a string *class* containing the following functions:

- Overloaded + operator function to carry out the concatenation of strings.
- Overloaded = (assignment) operator function to carry out string copy.
- Overloaded += operator function.
- Function to display the length of a string.
- Function to display the size of a string.
- Function *tolower( )* to convert upper case letters to lower case.
- Function *toupper( )* to convert lower case letters to upper case.

Ans

```
#include <iostream.h>
#include <string.h>

class string
{
    char * p ;

    public :

            string ( char *str = "" )
```

```
{
    p = new char [ strlen ( str ) + 1 ] ;
    strcpy ( p, str ) ;
}

string operator + ( string  s )
{
    char  *str = new char [ strlen ( p ) + strlen ( s.p ) + 1 ] ;
    strcpy ( str, p ) ;
    strcat ( str, s.p ) ;
    return string ( str ) ;
}

string operator = ( string  s )
{
    strcpy ( p, s.p ) ;
    return string ( p ) ;
}

string operator += ( string  s )
{
    char * temp = p ;
    p = new char [ strlen ( p ) + strlen ( s.p ) + 1 ] ;
    strcpy ( p, temp ) ;
    strcat ( p, s.p ) ;
    return string ( p ) ;
}

void toupper( )
{
    char * temp = p ;
    while ( *temp )
    {
        if ( *temp >= 'a' && *temp <= 'z' )
            *temp -= 32 ;
        temp++ ;
    }
}
```

```
            void tolower( )
            {
                char  * temp = p ;
                while ( *temp )
                {
                    if ( *temp >= 'A' && *temp <= 'Z' )
                        *temp += 32 ;
                    temp++ ;
                }
            }

            void showsize( )
            {
                cout << strlen ( p ) + 1 << endl ;
            }

            void showlength( )
            {
                cout << strlen ( p ) << endl ;
            }

            void display( )
            {
                cout << p << endl ;
            }
} ;

void main( )
{
    string  s = "Hi", s1 = "Hello", s2 ;
    s2 = s + s1 ;
    s += s1 ;
    s1 = s2 ;
    s1.toupper( ) ;
    s2.tolower( ) ;
    s.showsize( ) ;
    s.showlength( ) ;
    s.display( ) ;
```

```
        s1.display( ) ;
        s2.display( ) ;
}
```

Q 4.44

Functions defined in class are by default inline and those defined outside are not inline. How can we make them inline?

Ans

Functions can be made inline by writing the keyword *inline* in function's definition. This is shown in the following code:

```
class sample
{
    public :

        void fun( ) ;
};

inline void sample::fun( )
{
    // code
}
```

Q 4.45

How can one return an error value from the constructor?

Ans

An error value can never be returned from a constructor. However when a runtime error occurs, an exception can be thrown from within the constructor. Exceptions are discussed in Chapter 12.

Q 4.46

Why constructors do not have a return value?

Ans

Constructors are called whenever an object gets created. And there can never exist a situation where we want to return a value at the time of creation of an object.

Q 4.47

Can destructors be overloaded?

Ans

No. As we know, destructors are always called just before an object is about to die. There is no sense in passing any arguments to the destructor for the object whose death is certain.

Q 4.48

Can *delete* operator be overloaded?

Ans

Yes.

Q 4.49

State whether the following statements are True or False:

(a) Objects are to classes as variables are to data types.

Ans

True. The variables of the standard data types can be considered as instances of these data types, where each instance is likely to hold different data. Likewise, classes are user-defined data types from which objects can be instantiated. Each object is likely to hold different data. Hence each object is considered to hold a state.

(b) By default, members of a structure are *public* and that of a *class* are *private*.

Ans

True. Structures in C were used to combine dissimilar data types. In C++, they have been extended to hold functions but rest of their functionality has not been changed for backward compatibility. Hence, by default, their members are public. Most of the times, in C++ too, structures are used to create only user-defined data types with no functions in them.

As against this, to prevent unnecessary access (and thereby modification) of class data, its data members are, by default, *private*. However, the data must be accessible systematically through class member functions. These member functions are usually kept *public*.

(c) Nested classes are legal.

Ans

True. This is explained with the help of the following example:

```
class outer
{
        int i;

    public :

        class inner
        {
            float f;
        };
};

void main( )
{
```

```
        outer::inner  i ;
}
```

Here, class *inner* is declared inside the class *outer*. We cannot directly access the class *inner* from outside the class *outer*. To create an object of the *inner* class we must say *outer::inner i*. This too can be done only if the *inner* class is declared *public*. If it is declared *private* then it is not at all accessible from outside the *outer* class.

(d) In a *class*, data members are always *private*, whereas, member functions are always *public*.

Ans

False. Member functions can be *private* when we want that a function should be used only by the other member functions of that class. In rare situations data members can be kept *public*.

Usually data is kept *private* for two reasons:

- Access and modification to it can be controlled through member functions of the class.
- Data validation can be done before assigning values to data members. This is shown in the following example:

```
class sample
{
        int  data ;

    public :

        void setdata ( int  i )
        {
            if ( i > 0 )  // validate before assignment
                data = i ;
        }
```

```
};
```

(e) A class declaration creates space in memory for the members defined in it.

Ans

False. Memory space for the members of the class is allocated when an object of that class is created.

(f) It is necessary that a constructor in a *class* should always be *public*.

Ans

False. When we want that a user of the class should not be able to create an object of a class but the member functions of the class should be able to create it then the constructor should be made *private*. This is shown in the following example:

```
class sample
{
    private :

        int a ;

        sample ( int i )
        {
            a = i ;
        }

    public :

        sample( )
        {
        }

        void f( )
```

```
        {
              sample x ( 10 ) ;
        }
};

void main( )
{
    sample s1 ;  // works
    sample s2 ( 2 ) ;  // error
}
```

(g) Constructor is a member function of the *class*.

Ans

True. Even though a constructor is a member function of the class, it differs from other member functions in the following ways:

−   Constructor name should always be same as the class name. A function name can be any legal identifier.
−   Constructor does not have any return type. Functions always have some return type including *void*.
−   Constructor gets called automatically whenever an object gets created. Functions have to be called explicitly.

(h) If a *class* contains a three-argument constructor then it is necessary to define explicitly a zero-argument, a one-argument and a two-argument constructor.

Ans

The answer can be sometimes True and sometimes False.

True. If the class designer wants to allow creation of objects using zero-argument, one-argument & two-argument constructors. False, if he does not want to allow construction of such objects.

(i)   The compiler always provides a zero-argument constructor by default.

Ans

False. If we create an object using a zero-argument constructor and if the class does not contain the zero-argument constructor the compiler inserts one automatically. Note that the compiler inserts a default zero-argument constructor only if it does not find any other type of the constructor in the class. But if any other type of constructor is already defined then it becomes the class designer's responsibility to define the zero-argument constructor too, provided, he wants to allow creation of an object using a zero-argument constructor.

(j)   Member functions of a *class* have to be called explicitly, whereas, the constructor gets called automatically.

Ans

True. The object creation is a two step process. Firstly the memory is allocated and secondly its data members are initialized. For initialization, constructors are provided which always get called automatically. Member functions are used to modify, retrieve or print the data whenever required and hence are not called automatically.

(k)   Constructors can be overloaded.

Ans

True. Constructors are like other member functions of the class and hence can be overloaded. The only difference is that the constructors do not return any value.

(l)   Static memory allocation takes place during compilation, whereas, dynamic memory allocation takes place during execution.

Ans

True. The following code snippet shows the static as well as dynamic memory allocation:

Static memory allocation:

int i ;

Dynamic memory allocation:

int *i = (int*) malloc (sizeof (int)) ; // C style

Or

int *i = new int ; // C++ style

(m) Size of an object is equal to sum of sizes of data members and member functions within the *class*.

Ans

False. It seems that objects contain data members as well as member functions but physically they contain only data members and not the member functions. There is no need for an object to store member functions within it. This is because member functions do not change from one object to another. Since data members are used to hold data specific to objects they are different for different objects. The in-memory view of objects is as shown in the following figure:

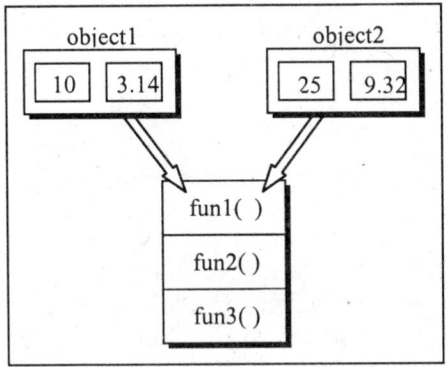

(n) When an object goes out of scope, its destructor gets called automatically.

Ans

True. Destructor is called just before the object is destroyed. It is used to do clean up operations like releasing dynamically allocated memory. This is shown in the following example:

```
#include <iostream.h>

class sample
{
        int *p ;

    public :

        sample ( int i )
        {
            p = new int ;
            *p = i ;
        }

        ~sample( )
        {
            delete p ;
```

```
        }
};

void main( )
{
    sample s ( 10 );
}
```

Here, when the object *s* is created its constructor gets called. In the constructor, memory is allocated dynamically and its base address is assigned to *p*. When *s* dies, *p* being a data member would also die. If the memory pointed by *p* is not released it would result in a memory leak. This is because *new* allocates memory on the heap and this memory is not released automatically. To avoid memory leak we should explicitly release the memory in the destructor.

(o) The *this* pointer always contains the address of the object using which the member function is being called.

Ans

True. Suppose *sample* is any user-defined class and we want to create multiple objects of this class, then each object would have its own copy of data members. The member functions of the class would work on these objects. Even though it appears that the member functions are the part of an object, physically they are not. The member functions of the class *sample* would be shared amongst all objects of the type *sample*. This is logical since member functions do not change for each object. Since the data members are used to hold values specific to an object they cannot be shared. This is shown in the following figure:

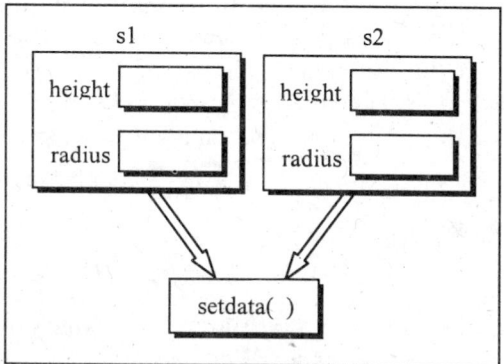

From this figure it is not clear how a member function comes to know which object's data members it has to access. This is explained with the help of following code:

```
class sample
{
        float  height, radius ;

    public :

        void setdata ( float  h, float  r )
        {
            height = h ;
            radius = r ;
        }
} ;

void main ( )
{
    sample  s1 ;
    sample  s2 ;

    s1.setdata ( 10.0f, 3.5f ) ;
    s1.setdata ( 5.0f, 2.5f ) ;
}
```

When *setdata( )* is called from *main( )* in addition to two parameters one more parameter gets passed to it implicitly. Through this parameter, address of the object using which *setdata( )* is called, gets passed. The *setdata( )* function collects this address in a special pointer called *this* pointer.

Hence the assignment statement in *setdata( )* now becomes,

```
this -> height = h ;
this -> radius = r ;
```

Thus, now there is no confusion as to which object's *height* and *radius* are being set. When *setdata( )* is called using *c1*, the *height* and *radius* of the object *c1* get set. Likewise, when *setdata( )* is called using *c2*, the *height* and *radius* of object *c2* get set.

(p) The *this* pointer can be used even in global functions.

Ans

False. The *this* pointer can be used only in the non-static member functions of the class.

(q) If the binary + operator is overloaded inside a *class* then, while calling it only one argument needs to be passed.

Ans

True. Let us take an example,

```
s = a + b ;
```

Here *s*, *a* and *b* are the objects of a class. The statement *a + b* would get expanded to *a.operator + (b)*. *a* is calling the member function *operator + ( )* with the parameter *b*. In the previous chapter since *operator + ( )* function was declared globally, the call to it was made in the following fashion:

```
operator + ( a, b ) ;
```

But if the function is a member of the class then the left-hand side operand calls it and the right hand side operand gets passed as an argument. And since the left-hand side operand calls the function, its address is passed to the *this* pointer. And using the *this* pointer the compiler identifies the data members of the object (left-hand side operand). For example, in the following function

```
complex operator + ( complex x )
{
    complex t;
    t.i = i + x.i;
    t.j = j + x.j;
    return t;
}
```

i and *j* would be treated as elements of the object *a*.

(r) If member functions of a *class* are defined outside the *class*, it is necessary to declare them inside the *class*.

Ans

True. Whenever the declaration and definition of a class are separated out, it is necessary to declare all the member functions within the class. This is to tell the compiler that these functions belong to the class but are defined somewhere outside the class. The way to declare and define the functions is as follows:

```
class sample
{
    public :

        int fun ( float f );
};

int sample :: fun ( float f )
{
```

```
        // code
    }   .
```

(s) We cannot modify the *this* pointer.

   Ans

   True. The *this* pointer being a *const* pointer cannot be modified.

Q 4.50

What would be the output of the following programs:

(a)
```cpp
#include <iostream.h>
class user
{
    private :

            int i ;
            float f ;
            char c ;

    public :

            void displaydata( )
            {
                cout << endl << i << '\n' << f << "\n" << c ;
            }
} ;

void main( )
{
    cout << sizeof ( user ) ;
    user u1 ;
    cout << endl << sizeof ( u1 ) ;
    u1.displaydata( ) ;
}
```

Ans

The output would be:

9 (under DOS) or 7 (under Windows)
9 (under DOS) or 7 (under Windows)
Garbage
Garbage
Garbage

Since the *user* class contains three elements: *int, float* and *char* its size would be 9 bytes (int-4, float-4, char-1) under Windows and 7 bytes (int-2, float-4, char-1) under DOS. Second output is again the same because *u1* is an object of the class *user*. Finally three garbage values are printed out because *i, f* and *c* are not initialized anywhere in the program.

Note that if you run this program you may not get the answer shown here. This is because packing is done for an object in memory for increasing the access efficiency. For example, under DOS, the object would be aligned on a 2-byte boundary. As a result, the size of the object would be reported as 6 bytes. Unlike this, Windows being a 32-bit OS the object would be aligned on a 4-byte boundary. Hence the size of the object would be reported as 12 bytes. To force the alignment on a 1-byte boundary, write the following statement before the class declaration.

#pragma pack (1)

(b)   #include <iostream.h>

```
class date
{
    private :

        int  dd, mm, yy ;

    public :
```

```
            date( )
            {
                cout << endl << "Reached here" ;
            }
    } ;

    void main( )
    {
        date  today ;
        date  *p = &today ;
        cout << endl << p ;
    }
```

Ans

The output would be:

```
Reached here
0X8F9C0FFA
```

The constructor of the class *date* is called when an object *today* gets created. The statement *cout*, which is present within the constructor, prints the message "Reached here". In *main( )* the address of *today* is stored in the pointer *p*. Hence the statement, *cout << endl << p* prints the address of *today*. When you run the program, the address may be different than the one displayed here.

(c)   #include <iostream.h>

```
    class student_rec
    {
        private :

                int  m1, m2, m3 ;
                float  percentage ;
```

```
    public :

        student_rec( )
        {
            m1 = m2 = m3 = 0 ;
            percentage = 0.0 ;
        }

        void calc_perc ( int  x, int  y , int  z )
        {
            m1 = x ; m2 = y ; m3 = z ;
            percentage = ( m1 + m2 + m3 ) / 3.0 ;
            display_perc( ) ;
        }

        void display_perc( )
        {
            cout << endl << "Percentage = " << percentage << "%" ;
        }
} ;

void main( )
{
    student_rec  s1 ;
    s1.display_perc( ) ;
    s1.calc_perc( 35, 35, 35 ) ;
    s1.display_perc( ) ;
}
```

Ans

The output would be:

Percentage = 0%
Percentage = 35%
Percentage = 35%
When $s1$ is created, the zero-argument constructor gets called where all data members are initialized with a value 0. Hence

when the function *aisplay_perc( )* is called through *s1*, it prints *Percentage = 0%*. Then the function *calc_perc( )* is called through *s1* by passing the values *35, 35, 35*. They are assigned to *m1*, *m2* and *m3* of *s1* and the percentage is calculated which is stored in the another data member *percentage*. Then there is a call to *display_perc( )* function from *calc_perc( )* which displays *Percentage = 35%*. Finally there is a call to *display_perc( )* through *s1* from *main( )* which once again prints *Percentage = 35%*. This program shows that the *public* member function (*display_perc( )*) can be called from within the class as well as from outside it.

(d)   ```
#include <iostream.h>

class control
{
    public :

        control( )
        {
            calculate( ) ;
            cout << endl << "Constructor" ;
        }

        void calculate( )
        {
            display( ) ;
            cout << endl << "Calculator" ;
        }
        void display( )
        {
            cout << endl << "displayed" ;
        }
} ;

void main( )
{
    control c1 ;
```
```

}

Ans

The output would be:

```
displayed
Calculator
Constructor
```

When object *c1* of the class *control* is created the constructor is called. The very first statement in the constructor is a call to *calculate( )*. From the function *calculate( )*, there is a call to *display( )* function where, through a *cout* a message is displayed. After displaying the message control returns from *display( )* to *calculate( )* where it prints the message "Calculator". Then control returns to the constructor of the class *control* where it prints the message "Constructor". Finally the control returns to *main( )* and since there are no more statements execution ends.

Q 4.51

Point out the errors, if any, in the following programs.

(a)
```
#include <string.h>
class address
{
    private :

        char name [ 10 ] ;
        char city [ 10 ] ;

    public :

        address ( char *p, char *q )
        {
            strcpy ( name, p ) ;
```

```
                    strcpy ( city, q ) ;
              }
      }

      //  main follows here
      void main( )
      {
          address my ( "Mac", "London" ) ;
      }
```

Ans

Error. Missing ';' after *class* definition.

(b)   class date

```
      {
          private :

              int  day, month, year ;

              date( )
              {
                  day = 25 ;
                  month = 9 ;
                  year = 1979 ;
              }
      };

      void main( )
      {
          date  today ;
      }
```

Ans

Error. While constructing the object of class *date* in *main( )*, it requires a zero-argument constructor. But the constructor is declared *private* and hence cannot be accessed from outside the *class*.

(c)
```
#include <iostream.h>
class triplets
{
    private :

        int t1, t2, t3 ;

    public :

        triplets ( int  x, int  y, int  z )
        {
            t1 = x ;
            t2 = y ;
            t3 = z ;
        }

        void display( )
        {
            cout << endl << t1 << t2 << t3 ;
        }
} ;

void main( )
{
    triplets  r ( 2, 3, 4 ), s ;
    r.display( ) ;
    s.display( ) ;
}
```

Ans

Error, because we are trying to create the object *s* using the zero-argument constructor which is not present in the class.

The compiler would not provide a zero-argument constructor, as a three-argument constructor already exists in the class.

(d) ```cpp
     #include <iostream.h>

     class sample
     {
         private :

             int data1 ;
             float data2 ;

         public :

             void sample( ) ;
             void displaydata( ) ;
     } ;

     void main( )
     {
         sample s ;
         s.showdata( ) ;
     }

     sample::void sample( )
     {
         data1 = 10 ;
         data2 = 20 ;
     }

     sample::void showdata( )
     {
         cout << endl << data1 << data2 ;
     }
     ```
     ```

Ans

Error. There are multiple errors in this program. The first error is in the declaration of the zero–argument constructor, whose return type is specified as *void*. The constructors never have a return type. The second error is in the definition of the constructor and the function *showdata( )*. Both are defined as *sample::void sample( )* and *sample::void showdata( )*, whereas, they should be defined in the following way:

```
void sample::sample( ) { }
void sample::showdata( ) { }
```

The third error is that there is no declaration of the *showdata( )* function in class *sample*.

(e)
```
#include <iostream.h>

class list
{
    private :

        class node
        {
            int  data ;
            node *link ;
        }*p ;

    public :

        void create( )
        {
            p = new node ;
            p.data = 10 ;
            p -> data = 10 ;
        }
};

void main( )
```

```
{
    list l1 ;
    l1.create( ) ;
}
```

Ans

Error. In the *create( )* function, *data* (which is a data member of the *node* class) has been accessed through *p* using a dot (.) operator. *p* being a pointer an -> operator should have been used.

(f)   class a
```
    {
        int i ;
    }

    main( )
    {
        // code
    }
```

Ans

No error. *Class a* is considered as return type of *main( )*.

5

The C++ Free Store

Q 5.1

Show the in-memory view of the memory allocated by the *new* operator.

Ans

Consider the following statement:

int *p = new int [5] ;

The in-memory view of the memory allocated by *new* is shown below.

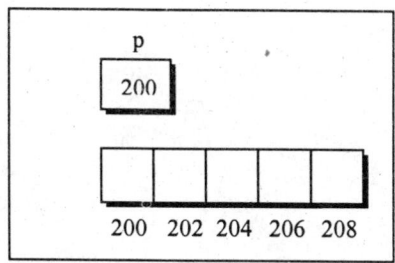

Q 5.2

If memory is allocated dynamically using *new* then can we expand the allocated memory using *realloc( )*?

Ans

Yes. This can be explained with the help of following example:

```
#include <iostream.h>
#include <malloc.h>

void main( )
{
    int *p = new int [ 5 ] ;
    p [ 1 ] = 3 ;
    p = ( int * ) realloc  ( p, sizeof ( int ) * 5 ) ;
    cout << p [ 1 ] ;
}
```

The *realloc( )* function expands the existing allocated memory if it finds enough contiguous memory locations that are required. If enough contiguous memory blocks are not available then the new memory block is allocated. The existing data is copied and the original memory block is freed.

Q 5.3

Can we apply *delete* on *this* pointer inside a member function?

Ans

Yes. If the member function has been called using pointer to an object, which is allocated dynamically, the object would get deleted. But if the member function has been called using the object, which is allocated statically, then a runtime error would occur. This is because we cannot call *delete* on statically allocated objects. This is shown in the following example:

```
class sample
{
        int i ;

    public :

        void fun( )
        {
            delete this ;
        }
} ;

void main( )
{
    sample *s = new sample ;
    s -> fun( ) ;  // no error

    sample s1 ;
    s1.fun( ) ;  // would throw a runtime error
}
```

Q 5.4

When would the memory be released if we have allocated it using *new* and not deleted it using *delete*?

Ans

If memory has been allocated using *new* and if it is not released by calling *delete* then it gets freed automatically when the program execution comes to an end.

Q 5.5

Does the expression *delete p* delete the pointer or the object being pointed to by *p*?

Ans

The expression *delete p* deletes the object being pointed to by *p*.

Q 5.6

How many bytes would be allocated by the following code?

```
#define MAXROW  3
#define MAXCOL  4

void main( )
{
    int ( *p ) [ MAXCOL ] ;
    p = new  int [ MAXROW ] [ MAXCOL ] ;
}
```

Ans

The memory allocated by the code is 24 bytes under DOS or 48 bytes under Windows. Here, total number of elements are 12 (3 rows and 4 columns). Each element would occupy 2 bytes under DOS and 4 bytes under Windows.

Q 5.7

Replace the following code using the *new* operator.

```
(a)  #include <malloc.h>

     #define MAXROW  3
     #define MAXCOL  4

     void main( )
     {
         int  ( *p )[ MAXCOL ] ;
         p = ( int ( * ) [ MAXCOL ] ) malloc ( MAXROW * sizeof ( *p ) ) ;
     }
```

Ans

```
#include <malloc.h>
#define MAXROW  3
#define MAXCOL  4

void main( )
{
    int  ( *p )[ MAXCOL ] ;
    p = new int [ MAXROW ] [ sizeof ( *p ) / sizeof ( int ) ] ;
}
```

(b) ```
#include <malloc.h>

#define MAXROW 3
#define MAXCOL 4

void main( )
{
    int (*p)[MAXROW][MAXCOL] ;
    p = (int (*) [MAXROW][MAXCOL]) malloc (sizeof (*p)) ;
}
```

**Ans**

```
#include <malloc.h>
#define MAXROW  3
#define MAXCOL  4

void main( )
{
    int  ( *p )[ MAXROW ][ MAXCOL ] ;
    p = new int [ 1 ] [ MAXROW ] [ MAXCOL ] ;
}
```

(c) ```
#include <malloc.h>

#define MAXROW 3
```

```
#define MAXCOL  4

void main( )
{
    int  **p, i ;
    p = ( int ** ) malloc ( MAXROW * sizeof ( int * ) ) ;
    for ( i = 0 ; i < MAXROW ; i++ )
        p [ i ] = ( int * ) malloc ( MAXCOL * sizeof ( int ) ) ;
}
```

Ans

```
#include <malloc.h>
#define MAXROW  3
#define MAXCOL  4

void main( )
{
    int  **p, i ;
    p = new int* [ MAXROW ] ;

    for ( i = 0 ; i < MAXROW ; i++ )
        p [ i ] = new int [ MAXCOL ] ;
}
```

(d) ```
#include <malloc.h>

#define MAXROW 3
#define MAXCOL 4

void main( )
{
    int **p, i ;
    p = (int **) malloc (MAXROW * sizeof (int *)) ;
    p [0] = (int *) malloc (MAXROW * MAXCOL * sizeof (int)) ;

    for (i = 0 ; i < MAXROW ; i++)
        p [i] = p [0] + i * MAXCOL ;
```
```

```
}
```

Ans

```
#include <malloc.h>
#define MAXROW  3
#define MAXCOL  4

void main( )
{
    int **p, i, j ;
    p = new int* [ MAXROW ] ;

    p [ 0 ] = new int [ MAXROW * MAXCOL ] ;

    for ( i = 0 ; i < MAXROW ; i++ )
        p [ i ] = p [ 0 ] + i * MAXCOL ;
}
```

Q 5.8

State whether the following statements are True or False:

(a) If memory is allocated using *new [ ]* it must be deallocated using *delete [ ]*.

Ans

True. When memory is allocated using *new[ ]* if we use only *delete* to deallocate it, it deletes the complete array. But if the array is an array of objects, then the destructor is called only for the first object in the array. Whereas, on using *delete[ ]*, it deletes the complete array and calls the destructor for each object in the array.

(b) *new* not only allocates memory but also calls the object's constructor.

Ans

True. *new* and *malloc( )* both are used to allocate memory. The major difference between these two is that *malloc( )* does not call the constructor but *new* does.

(c) Heap and free store are two different things.

Ans

False. While using *new*, memory is allocated from the heap. In C++, heap is also known as a free store.

(d) Deleting a NULL pointer is safe and is guaranteed to do nothing.

Ans

True. If the *delete* operator is used on the pointer containing NULL in it, no memory is deallocated.

(e) In C++ to reallocate memory we should use the *renew* operator.

Ans

False. There is no such operator called *renew* in C++ like the *realloc( )* function in C.

(f) The *new* operator always returns a pointer of appropriate type, whereas, *malloc( )* returns a *void* pointer which needs to be typecast explicitly.

Ans

True. The *new* operator does the typecasting internally.

(g) Like other operators the *new* operator can also be overloaded.

Ans

True. We can overload the *new* operator if we want to enhance the capability of it, like initializing the allocated memory with a value 25. This is shown in the following program:

```
#include <iostream.h>
#include <malloc.h>

void * operator new ( size_t s, int i )
{
    int *q = ( int * ) malloc ( s ) ;
    *q = i ;
    return q ;
}

void main( )
{
    int *p = new ( 25 ) int ;
    cout << *p ;
    delete p ;
}
```

(h) We should never *delete* a pointer twice.

Ans

True. When the pointer is deleted for the first time, the address pointed to by the pointer is freed and returned back to the heap. Then, if we again delete the same pointer, the remains of what used to be an object are passed to the destructor (which could be disastrous), and the memory pointed to by the pointer is handed back to the heap a second time. This may corrupt the heap.

(i) _new_handler is a pointer to a function provided by C++ for managing free store exhaustion.

Ans

True. Usually, *_new_handler* pointer contains NULL, and when *new* fails to allocate memory, *new* returns NULL. But if the *_new_handler* function pointer contains a non-null value, then when *new* fails to allocate memory it transfers the control to the function being pointed to by the *_new_handler*.

(j) We can overload the *new* and *delete* operators on a global basis as well as on a class by class basis.

Ans

True. The following example shows how to overload *new* and *delete* operators on global basis:

```
#include <iostream.h>
#include <malloc.h>

void * operator new ( size_t  s )
{
    void  *q = malloc ( s ) ;
    return  q ;
}

void operator delete ( void  *q )
{
    free ( q ) ;
}

void main( )
{
    int  *p = new int ;
    *p = 25 ;
    cout << *p ;
    delete  p ;
}
```

The following example shows how to overload *new* and *delete* operators on class by class basis:

```cpp
#include <iostream.h>
#include <malloc.h>

class sample
{
        int i ;
        char c ;

    public :

        void* operator new ( size_t s, int ii, char cc )
        {
            sample *q = ( sample * ) malloc ( s ) ;
            q -> i = ii ;
            q -> c = cc ;
            return q ;
        }

        void operator delete ( void *q )
        {
            free ( q ) ;
        }

        void display( )
        {
            cout << i << "\t" << c ;
        }
};

class sample1
{
        float f ;

    public :
```

```
                    void* operator new ( size_t s, float ff )
                    {
                        sample1 *q = ( sample1 * ) malloc ( s ) ;
                        q -> f = ff ;
                        return q ;
                    }

                    void operator delete ( void *q )
                    {
                        free ( q ) ;
                    }

                    void show( )
                    {
                        cout << endl << f ;
                    }
            } ;

    void main( )
    {
        sample *s = new ( 7, 'a' ) sample ;
        s -> display( ) ;
        delete s ;

        sample1 *s1 = new ( 5.6f ) sample1 ;
        s1 -> show( ) ;
        delete s1 ;
    }
```

Operator *new* is overloaded whenever we want to initialize the allocated memory with some value. When the operator *new* is overloaded on global basis it becomes impossible to initialize the data members of a class as different classes have different types of data members.

Overloading the operator *new* on class by class basis can solve this problem. This is because we can now overload *new* in each class separately and accept values in the overloaded operator function according to data members to be initialized.

(k) In one class the *delete* operator can be overload only once.

Ans

True.

(l) The object created using *new* does not get destroyed when the control returns from the function in which it was created.

Ans

True. Any dynamically allocated memory is destroyed only when it is explicitly released or when the program comes to an end. So even if the pointer that holds the address of the allocated memory dies, the object pointed to by pointer is not destroyed. This is shown in the following code:

```
#include <iostream.h>

struct data
{
    int i ;
    float f ;
} ;

void fun( )
{
    data *q = new data ;
}

void main( )
{
    fun( ) ;
    // code
}
```

When the function *fun( )* gets called from *main( )* memory is allocated for the object of the type *data* and its address gets assigned to *q*. As soon as the control returns from the function *fun( )*, the local pointer variable *q* dies. But the object would continue to exists until it is explicitly deallocated or the program ends.

(m) The *this* pointer can be used in a class specific overloaded *new* operator function.

Ans

False. The *this* pointer is never passed to the overloaded *operator new( )* member function because this function gets called before the object is created. Hence there is no question of the *this* pointer getting passed to *operator new( )*.

(n) Memory cannot be dynamically allocated for references.

Ans

True. The references are initialized at the time of creation. Trying to allocate memory dynamically for a reference creates a problem in initializing it. Thus, the compiler does not allow us to dynamically allocate the memory for references.

(o) It is unsafe to deallocate the memory using *free( )* if it has been allocated using *new*.

Ans

True. This is explained with the help of following example:

```
#include <malloc.h>

class sample
{
        int *p ;
```

```
        public :

            sample( )
            {
                p = new int ;
            }

            ~sample( )
            {
                delete p ;
            }
};

void main( )
{
    sample *s1 = new sample ;
    free ( s1 ) ;

    sample *s2 = ( sample * ) malloc ( sizeof ( sample ) ) ;
    delete s2 ;
}
```

The *new* operator allocates memory and calls the constructor. In the constructor we have allocated memory on heap which is pointed to by *p*. If we release the object using the *free( )* function the object would die but the memory allocated in the constructor would leak. This is because *free( )* being a C library function does not call the destructor where we have deallocated the memory.

As against this, if we allocate memory by calling *malloc( )* the constructor would not get called. Hence *p* holds a garbage address. Now if the memory is deallocated using *delete*, the destructor would get called where we have tried to release the memory pointed to by *p*. Since *p* contains garbage this may result in a runtime error.

Q 5.9

What will be the output of the following program?

```
#include <iostream.h>
#define MAXROW  3
#define MAXCOL  4

void main( )
{
    int ( *p ) [ MAXCOL ] ;
    p = new int [ MAXROW ] [ MAXCOL ] ;
    cout << endl << sizeof ( p ) << endl << sizeof ( *p ) ;
}
```

Ans

The output would be:

2 (under DOS) or 4 (under Windows)
8 (under DOS) or 16 (under Windows)

Here, *p* is a pointer to an array of 4 elements. *sizeof (p)* would give us the size of the pointer *p*. *p* being a *near* pointer, it would be 2 bytes under DOS, and 4 bytes under Windows.

We have made *p* to point to a 2D array. So **p* would point to the first 1D array. Hence *sizeof (*p)* would give the size of the first 1D array which would be 8 bytes under DOS or 16 bytes under Windows.

Q 5.10

Point out the errors, if any, in the following program.

```
#include <iostream.h>
#include <stdlib.h>
#include <new.h>

void main( )
```

```
{
    void memwarning( ) ;
    _new_handler = warning ;

    char *p ;
    p = new char [ 64000u ] ;
}

void warning( )
{
    cout << endl << "Free store has now gone empty" ;
    exit ( 1 ) ;
}
```

Ans

Error. *_new_handler* is a pointer to a user-defined function, which is used to display error messages, and is not accessible. Its value is set through the function *set_new_handler( )*. But here we are trying to set the value of *_new_handler* directly by assigning it an address of a function, which results in an error. Another error is that the prototype of function *warning( )* is not mentioned before the call.

Q 5.11

Point out the logical error, if any, in the following program.

```
#include <iostream.h>

class sample
{
    private :

        int *p ;

    public :
```

```
         sample( )
         {
                 p = new  int ;
         }
};

void main( )
{
     sample  s ;
}
```

Ans

Ideally if any memory is allocated dynamically in the constructor it must be deallocated in the destructor. But, here it has not been deallocated.

Q 5.12

Write a program that will allocate memory for a 1-D, 2-D and a 3-D array of integers. Store some values in these arrays and then print them out. We must be able to access elements of these arrays using forms *a[i], b[i][j]* and *c[i][j][k]*.

Ans

The program is as follows:

```
#include <iostream.h>

void main( )
{
    int *a1 = new int [ 5 ] ;
    int ( *a2 ) [ 2 ] = new int [ 2 ] [ 2 ] ;
    int ( *a3 ) [ 2 ] [ 2 ] = new int [ 2 ] [ 2 ] [ 2 ] ;

    int i, j, k, l ;
```

```
for ( i = 0 ; i <= 4 ; i++ )
    a1 [ i ] = i ;

for ( k = i = 0 ; i <= 1 ; i++ )
    for ( j = 0 ; j <= 1 ; j++ )
        a2 [ i ] [ j ] = ++k ;

for ( l = i = 0 ; i <= 1 ; i++ )
    for ( j = 0 ; j <= 1 ; j++ )
        for ( k = 0 ; k <= 1 ; k++ )
            a3 [ i ] [ j ] [ k ] = ++l ;

cout << "1-D array is : " << endl ;
for ( i = 0 ; i <= 4 ; i++ )
    cout << a1 [ i ] << "\t" ;

cout << endl << endl ;
cout << "2-D array is : " << endl ;

for ( i = 0 ; i <= 1 ; i++ )
{
    for ( j = 0 ; j <= 1 ; j++ )
        cout << a2 [ i ] [ j ] << "\t" ;
    cout << endl ;
}

cout << endl ;
cout << "3-D array is : " << endl ;
for ( i = 0 ; i <= 1 ; i++ )
    for ( j = 0 ; j <= 1 ; j++ )
    {
        for ( k = 0 ; k <= 1 ; k++ )
            cout << a3 [ i ] [ j ] [ k ] << "\t" ;
        cout << endl ;
    }
}
```

The output would be:

1-D array is :
0   1   2   3   4

2-D array is :
1   2
3   4

3-D array is :
1   2
3   4
5   6
7   8

Miscellaneous Class Issues

How to initialize the static data?

Ans

The *static* data is always defined outside the class but its declaration is done inside the class. We can initialize the static data member either when it is defined or in the constructor. This is shown in the following code:

```
#include <iostream.h>

class sample
{
        static int i ; // declaration

    public :

        sample ( int ii = 0 )
```

```
              {
                  i = ii ;  // initialization
              }

              void show( )
              {
                  cout << i ;
              }
};

int sample::i = 8 ;  // definition and initialization

void main( )
{
    sample s ( 25 ) ;
    s.show( ) ;
}
```

Q 6.2

Can a non-static member function access the static data?

Ans

Yes. The non-static member function works on objects as well as on *static* data members.

Q 6.3

Can user-defined object be declared as static data member of another class?

Ans

Yes. This following code shows how to initialize a user-defined object.

```
#include <iostream.h>
```

```
class test
{
        int i ;

    public :

        test ( int ii = 0 )
        {
            i = ii ;
        }
};

class sample
{
        static test s ;
};

test sample::s ( 26 ) ;
```

Here we have initialized the object *s* by calling the one-argument constructor. We can use the same convention to initialize the object by calling multiple-argument constructor.

Q 6.4

How do I initialize a *const* data member?

Ans

This is shown in the following example:

```
#include <iostream.h>

class sample
{
        const int t ;

    public :
```

```
            sample ( int  i ) : t ( i )
            {
            }
};

void main( )
{
     sample  s ( 25 ) ;
}
```

Here, *t* is the *const* data member of the class *sample*. When an object *s* is created, 25 is passed to the one-argument constructor. It gets collected in parameter *i* which is then assigned to *t*. It is necessary to initialize the *const* data member in the definition of the constructor as shown in the program.

Q 6.5

In which of the following cases can we use *const*:

– On normal variables
– On function arguments
– On member functions of a class
– On member function arguments
– On objects

Ans

The *const* qualifier can be used in all the given cases.

Q 6.6

If we wish to provide an assignment operator and a copy constructor within a class called *rectangle* what would be their prototypes?

Ans

```
rectangle operator = ( rectangle  r ) ;  // assignment operator
rectangle ( rectangle  &r ) ;  // copy constructor
```

Q 6.7

What do we gain by declaring the data member as *const*?

Ans

Once the *const* data members are initialized they cannot be changed. Hence the known constants such as value of PI, gravitational force, etc. that never change should be declared as *const*.

Q 6.8

Explain with a figure how static data is shared amongst objects of the class?

Ans

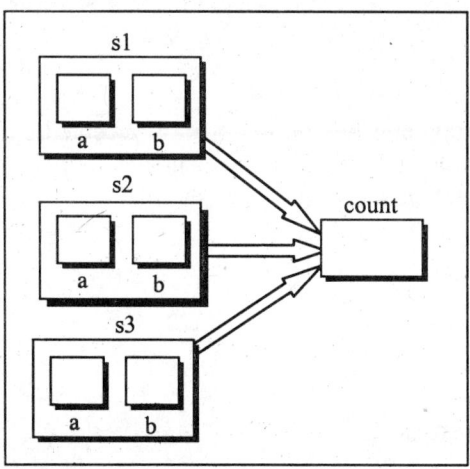

Here *s1*, *s2* and *s3* are the objects of a class. *count* is a *static* data member of the same class. Hence it is being shared amongst the three objects, whereas, *a* and *b* are non-static data members and hence each object has a different copy of them.

Q 6.9

Is there a concept of *const* classes in C++?

Ans

No.

Q 6.10

What is the difference between a copy constructor and an assignment operator?

Ans

Refer Q 6.12 (m)

Q 6.11

Is it necessary to accept a reference in the copy constructor?

Ans

Yes. If in the copy constructor an object is accepted by value then the copy constructor will fall in a recursive loop. This can be explained with the help of following example:

```
class sample
{
      int i ;

   public :

      sample ( sample p )
      {
          i = p.i ;
      }
};

void main( )
```

```
{
    sample s ;
    sample s1 ( s );
}
```

When the statement *sample s1 (s)* is executed, the copy constructor gets called. If the copy constructor accepts the value, then the value of *s* would be passed which would get collected in *p*. We can think of this statement as *sample p = s*. Here *p* is getting created and initialized. Hence again the copy constructor would get called. This would result into recursive calls.

Q 6.12

State whether the following statements are True or False:

(a) A *static* data member is useful when all objects of a class are to share a common item of information.

Ans

True. While programming there are situations where some data needs to be shared amongst all objects of a class. In such situations the data must be declared as *static*. For example, in a *calendar* class the variable that stores name of the months can be shared amongst objects and hence should be made *static*.

The *static* data member is also useful if we want to count the number of objects that are instantiated from the class. (To count number of objects we would have to declare a data member as *static* and have to increment it in the constructor.)

(b) If a class has a *static* data member and three objects are created from this class, then each object would have its own *static* data member.

Ans

False. There would be only one copy of the *static* data member, which would be shared amongst all objects of that class.

(c) A class can have *static* data members as well as *static* member functions.

Ans

True. Whenever there is a requirement that a function of a class needs to be called without using an object then the function must be declared as *static*.

The *static* member functions can operate only upon *static* data members.

(d) A *static* data member's definition appears in the class declaration, but the variable is actually declared outside the class.

Ans

False. A *static* data member is declared inside the class but its definition always appears outside the class. This is because, if *static* data members were defined inside the class declaration, it would violate the idea that a class declaration is only the blueprint and does not set aside any memory. Defining the static member data outside the class also emphasizes two facts:

– The memory space for such data is allocated only once, before the program starts executing.
– There is only one static member variable for all the objects of a class; each object does not have its own version of the variable.

(e) If *display( )* is a *static* member function of a class called *sample* then it can be called in the following way:

```
sample s1 ;
s1.display( ) ;
```

Ans

True. The *static* member function never operates upon objects and so there is no need of any object to call it. It is usually called using the class name. But even if it is called using an object it is an acceptable syntax.

(f) If *display( )* is a *static* member function of a class called *sample* then it can be called in the following way:

```
sample::display( ) ;
```

Ans

True.

(g) The *const* can be used on member functions of a class as well as on member function arguments.

Ans

True. The *const* member functions are used to prevent modification of class data members within it. Likewise, the *const* parameters are used to prevent modification of data collected by them. This is shown in the following program:

```
class sample
{
        int i ;

    public :

        // const member function
```

```
        int fun( ) const
        {
            i = 82 ;  // error
            return  i ;
        }

        // const function argument
        void fun1 ( const int  &ii )
        {
            ii = 8 ;  // error
        }
};

void main( )
{
    sample  s ;
    int  p = 9 ;
    p = s.fun( ) ;
    s.fun1 ( p ) ;
}
```

Here *fun( )* is a *const* member function. Hence, compiler flashes an error when we try to modify the data member *i*. Similarly, the function *fun1( )* cannot modify the value of *ii* as *ii* is declared as *const*.

(h) A *const* member function prevents modification of any of its class's member data.

Ans

True.

(i) If a member function of a class is to be *const* then it is necessary to use *const* in declaration as well as in definition of the member function.

Ans

True. For example,

```
class sample
{
        int i ;

    public :

        int fun( ) const  ;
};

int sample::fun( ) const
{
    return i ;
}.
```

(j) You can use only *const* member functions with *const* objects.

Ans

True. The value of *const* objects should not change in any case. If a non-*const* member function is called upon it, the member function might change its data. Hence C++ allows us to call only the *const* member functions using the *const* objects.

(k) If we don't provide an assignment operator in a class declaration then the compiler automatically adds one to our class.

Ans

True. Assignment is a basic operation and hence the overloaded assignment operator should be available in all the classes. For example,

```
class twowheeler
```

```
{
    private :

        char  type [ 20 ] ;

    public :

        // member functions
} ;

void main( )
{
    twowheeler o1 ( "Bike" ), o2 ;
    o2 = o1 ;
}
```

In this program if each object represents a particular type of two-wheeler then we might have two objects consisting the same type of two-wheelers. At such a time we would assign the value of one object to another. Assignment being the basic operation, compiler always provides an overloaded assignment operator to all classes.

(l)   If we don't provide a copy constructor in a class declaration then the compiler automatically adds one.

Ans

True. The copy constructor is used to copy an object into another of the same type at the time of initialization. Hence it gets called when an object is passed to a function or returned from a function by value. So the compiler by default always provides a copy constructor in a class.

(m) The following two sets of statements are same:

```
sample s1 ;
s1 = s2 ;
```

and

sample s1 = s2 ;

Ans

False. In the first set, *s1* gets created. Then *s1* is assigned a value of *s2* through an assignment operator.

In the second set, *s1* gets created. Then *s1* is initialized with a value of *s2* through the copy constructor.

(n) When an object is passed to a function by value or returned from a function by value the copy constructor gets called.

Ans

True. This can be explained with the help of following example:

```
#include <iostream.h>

class sample
{
    public :

        sample( )
        {
        }

        sample ( sample &s ) // copy constructor
        {
            cout << "copy" << endl ;
        }

        sample fun ( sample s )
        {
            sample t ;
            t = s ;
```

```
                return t ;
            }
};

void main( )
{
    sample  s1, s2, s3 ;
    s3 = s1.fun ( s2 ) ;
}
```

The above program gives the output as:

```
copy
copy
```

Copy constructor gets called when an object needs to be initialized with the value of another object of the same type.

From the output of this program it is clear that the copy constructor gets called twice. Firstly when the *fun( )* function collects the value of *s2* in the formal argument *s*. We can think of this statement as *sample s = s2*. Here *s2* is getting created and initialized.

Secondly the copy constructor gets called when the value of *t* is returned from the function *fun( )*. To collect the value of *t* a nameless object gets created and initialized.

(o) To carry out conversion from an object to a basic type or vice-versa it is necessary to provide the conversion functions.

Ans

True. As the compiler does not have the knowledge of the user-defined class, the conversion operators are necessary to carry out the conversion from one type to another. The conversion operators have been already discussed in the chapter on "Classes In C++".

(p)   To carry out conversion from object of one type to another it is necessary to provide the conversion functions.

Ans

True. Let us understand how to perform conversion from one user-defined type to another.

```
class circle
{
    private :

        int  radius ;

    public :

        circle ( int  r = 0 )
        {
            radius = r ;
        }
} ;

class rectangle
{
    private :

        int  length, breadth  ;

    public :

        rectangle ( int  l,  int  b )
        {
            length = l ;
            breadth = b ;
        }

        operator circle( )
        {
            return circle ( length ) ;
```

```
        }
};

void main( )
{
    rectangle r ( 20, 10 ) ;
    circle  c ;
    c = r ;
}
```

When *c = r* is executed the compiler searches for an overloaded assignment operator in the class *circle* which accepts the object of type *rectangle*. Since there is no such overloaded assignment operator, the conversion operator function that converts the *rectangle* object to the *circle* object is searched in the *rectangle* class. We have provided such a conversion operator in the *rectangle* class. This is shown below.

```
operator circle( )
{
    return circle ( length ) ;
}
```

This conversion operator function returns a *circle* object. By default conversion operators have the name and return type same as the object type to which it converts to. Here the type of the object is *circle* and hence the name of the operator function as well as the return type is *circle*.

(q) The *this* pointer can be used inside non-static member functions as well as in static member functions.

Ans

False. The *this* pointer cannot be used inside the *static* member function. This is because the *static* member functions are always called through the class name and not through the objects.

Q 6.13

Point out the errors, if any, in the following programs.

(a)
```cpp
#include <iostream.h>
class sample
{
    private :

        static int  count ;

    public :

        sample( )
        {
            count = 10 ;
        }

        void display( ) const
        {
            cout << endl << "count = " << count ;
        }
};

void main( )
{
    sample  s1, s2, s3 ;
    s1. display ( ) ;
    s2. display ( ) ;
    s3. display ( ) ;
}
```

Ans

Error. The *static* data members are always defined outside the class. Here, *count* is a static data member of the class *sample* and it is not defined. The way to define it is as follows:

```
class sample
{
    // code
};

int  sample::count ;
```

(b)   #include <iostream.h>

```
class example
{
    private :

        int  data ;

    public :

        example( ) ;
        void display( ) const ;
};

example::example( )
{
    data = 0 ;
}

example::display( )
{
    cout << endl << "data = " << data ;
}

void main( )
{
```

```
        example  d ;
        d.display( ) ;
}
```

Ans

Error. According to the declaration of the .function *display( )*
the definition of the *display( )* function should be as follows:

```
void example::display( ) const
{
    // code
}
```

Q 6.14

Write a program that consists of two classes *time12* and *time24*.
The first one maintains time on a 12-hour basis, whereas the other
one maintains it on a 24-hour basis. Provide conversion functions
to carry out the conversion from object of one type to another.

Ans

Following is the program that implements the conversion operator
functions.

```
class time24 ;  // forward reference

class time12
{
        int  hour ;
        int  minute ;
        int  second ;

    public :

        time12 ( int  h, int  m, int  s ) ;
        operator time24( ) ;
} ;
```

```
class time24
{
        int  hour ;
        int  minute ;
        int  second ;

    public :

        time24 ( int  h, int  m, int  s ) ;
        operator time12( ) ;
} ;

time12::time12 ( int  h, int  m, int  s )
{
    hour = h ;
    minute = m ;
    second = s ;
}

time12::operator time24( )
{
    time12  t ( hour, minute, second ) ;
    return t ;
}

time24::time24 ( int  h, int  m, int  s )
{
    hour = h ;
    minute = m ;
    second = s ;
}

time24::operator time12( )
{
    time12  t ( hour, minute, second ) ;
    return t ;
}
```

```
void main( )
{
    time12  a ( 11, 23, 45 ) ;
    time24  b ( 10, 35, 23 ) ;
    a = b ;
    b = a ;
}
```

In this program there are two classes—*time12* and *time24*. In both the classes there are conversion functions that convert the objects into the other type.

This program uses a forward reference for the class *time24* because *time12* uses the *time24* class and vice-versa.

Q 6.15

Write a program that implements a *date* class containing data members *day*, *month* and *year*. Implement assignment operator and copy constructor in this class.

Ans

```
#include <iostream.h>

class date
{
        int  day ;
        int  month ;
        int  year ;

    public :

        date ( int  d = 0, int  m = 0, int  y = 0 )
        {
            day = d ;
            month = m ;
            year = y ;
```

```
        }

        // copy constructor
        date ( date  &d )
        {
            day = d.day ;
            month = d.month ;
            year = d.year ;
        }

        // overloaded assignment operator
        date operator = ( date  d )
        {
            day = d.day ;
            month = d.month ;
            year = d.year ;
            return  d ;
        }

        void display( )
        {
            cout << day << "/" << month << "/" << year ;
        }
};

void main( )
{
    date  d1 ( 25, 9, 1979 ) ;
    date  d2 = d1 ;
    date  d3 ;
    d3 = d2 ;
    d3.display( ) ;
}
```

Q 6.16

Design a class from which only one object can be created. If more than one object is created the program should terminate.

Ans

The class of which only one object can be created is known as a singleton class. The following program defines a singleton class *sample*.

```
#include <process.h>
#include <iostream.h>

class sample
{
        static int count ;

    public :

        sample( )
        {
            if ( count == 1 )
                exit ( 0 ) ;
            count++ ;
        }
} ;

int sample::count = 0 ;

void main( )
{
    sample s1 ;
    sample s2 ;
}
```

In *main( )* we have created two objects. As soon as the second object is created the program terminates.

Inheritance

Q 7.1

Assume a class *D* that is *privately* derived from class *B*. Which of the following can an object of class *D* located in *main( )* access?

- *public* members of *D*
- *protected* members of *D*
- *private* members of *D*
- *public* members of *B*
- *protected* members of *B*
- *private* members of *B*

Ans

Only the *public* members of the class *D* are accessible through an object of class *D* from *main( )*.

Q 7.2

When does an ambiguity occur in multiple inheritance?

Ans

This can be explained with the help of following example:

```
class base1
{
    public :

        void fun( )
        {
            // code
        }
};

class base2
{
    public :

        void fun( )
        {
            // code
        }
};

class derived : public base1, public base2
{
    // code
};

void main( )
{
    derived d ;
    d.fun( ) ;
}
```

When the function *fun( )* is called using the object *d* of derived class, it results in an ambiguity because the compiler is unable to decide which *fun( )* function should be called, the one which belongs to class *base1* or the one which belongs to class *base2*.

Q 7.3

State whether the following statements are True or False:

(a) We can derive a class from a base class even if the base class's source code is not available.

Ans

True. To derive a class from a base class we need to have the base class's declaration. The declaration is generally present in the header files.

(b) Multiple inheritance is different from multiple levels of inheritance.

Ans

True. Multiple inheritance means deriving a class from more than one classes. On the other hand, multiple levels of inheritance means a class has been derived from a base class and the base class itself has been derived from another base class.

(c) The way a derived class member function can access base class *protected* and *public* members, the base class member functions can access *protected* and *public* member functions of derived class.

Ans

False. Base class cannot access derived class members since it does not have any knowledge of the derived class.

(d) It is possible to derive a class through *public* derivation, *private* derivation or *protected* derivation.

Ans

True.

(e) A derived class member function has an access to *protected* and *public* members of base class, irrespective of whether the derived class has been derived *public*ly or *private*ly.

Ans

True. When a class is *public*ly derived from a base class then *protected* and *public* members of the base class remain same for the derived class.

When a class is *private*ly derived from a base class then the *protected* and *public* members of the base class become *private* members for the derived class.

When a class is *protected*ly derived from a base class then the *protected* and *public* members of the base class become *protected* members for the derived class.

(f) If the derived class has been derived *public*ly then a derived class object, can access *public* members of base class.

Ans

True. Refer (e) above.

(g) An object of a derived class (however derived) cannot access *private* or *protected* members of base class.

Ans

True. The *private* members of the base class are never accessible outside the class. The *protected* members of the base class are accessible only to the derived classes.

(h) *private* members of base class cannot be accessed by derived class member functions or objects of derived class.

Ans

True.

(i) In public inheritance the *protected* members of the base class become *public* for the functions outside the derived class.

Ans

False.

(j) There is no difference between *private* and *protected* inheritance.

Ans

False. This can be explained with the help of the following example:

Private Inheritance	Protected Inheritance

class base
{
    private :
        int pri ;
    protected :
        int pro ;
    public :
        int pub ;
} ;
 	
class der1 : private base
{
} ;
 	
class der2 : public der1
{
} ;
	class base
	{
	    private :
	        int pri ;
	    protected :
	        int pro ;
	    public :
	        int pub ;
	} ;
	
	class der1 : protected base
	{
	} ;
	
	class der2 : public der1
	{
	} ;

Case: *private* Inheritance

Since the class *der1* is *private*ly derived, the *pri*, *pro* and *pub* data members become *private* for the class *der1*. Hence they are not available to the *der2* class.

Case: *protected* Inheritance

Since the class *der1* is *protected*ly derived, the *pri*, *pro* and *pub* data members become *protected* for the class *der1*. Hence they are available to the *der2* class.

(k)   In *private* inheritance part of the base class interface can be made available to the functions outside the derived class.

   Ans

   True. When we inherit privately all *public* members of the base class become *private* for the derived class. If we want only some of them to remain *private* and the rest to be accessible from outside the derived class it can be done as shown in the following example:

```
class base
{
    public :

        void fun1( )
        {
            // code
        }

        void fun2( )
        {
            // code
        }
};

class derived : private base
{
```

```
        public :

            base::fun2 ;
    } ;

    void main( )
    {
        derived  d ;
        d.fun2( ) ;  // works
        d.fun1( ) ;  // error
    }
```

Here the function *fun2( )* is accessible from *main( )* in spite of *private* inheritance. This is achieved just by mentioning the name (no arguments or return values) of the function *fun2( )* as *base::fun2* in the public section of the derived class. *fun1( )* is not accessible from *main( )*. Similarly, we can make a member *private* if the derived class is *public*ly derived.

(l)   The size of a derived class object is equal to the sum of sizes of data members in base class and the derived class.

    Ans

    True.

(m) Creating a derived class from a base class requires fundamental changes to the base class.

    Ans

    False.

(n) If a base class contains a member function *func( )*, and a derived class does not contain a function with this name, an object of the derived class cannot access *func( )*.

Ans

False. It depends upon how the function *func( )* has been defined in the base class and also on how the class has been derived. If the function *func( )* is defined *public* in base class and the derived class has been derived *public*ly then an object of the derived class can access the function *func( )*.

(o) If a base class and a derived class each include a member function with the same name, the member function of the derived class will be called by an object of the derived class

Ans

True. This is because the member functions are always searched in the derived class and then in the base class.

(p) A class *D* can be derived from a class *C*, which is derived from a class *B*, which is derived from a class *A*.

Ans

True. This is known as multiple levels of inheritance.

(q) It is illegal to make objects of one class as members of another class.

Ans

False.

Q 7.4

What will be the output of the following programs:

(a)
```
#include <iostream.h>
class base
{
    private :
```

```
        int i ;
};

class derived : public base
{
    private :

        int j ;
};

void main( )
{
    cout << endl << sizeof ( derived ) << endl << sizeof ( base ) ;
    derived o1 ;
    base o2 ;
    cout << endl << sizeof ( o1 ) << endl << sizeof ( o2 ) ;
}
```

Ans

The output would be:

4 (under DOS) or 8 (under Windows)
2 (under DOS) or 4 (under Windows)
4 (under DOS) or 8 (under Windows)
2 (under DOS) or 4 (under Windows)

The size of class depends upon the sizes of its non-static data members. The size of a derived class is sum of the sizes of non-static data members of the base class and the derived class.

(b) #include <iostream.h>

```
class base1
{
    private :

        int b1 ;
```

```
};

class base2
{
    private :

        int b2 ;
};

class derived : public base1, public base2
{
    private :

        int d1 ;
};

void main( )
{
    cout << endl << sizeof ( base1 ) << endl << sizeof ( base2 )
        << endl << sizeof ( derived ) ;
}
```

Ans

The output would be:

2 (under DOS) or 4 (under Windows)
2 (under DOS) or 4 (under Windows)
6 (under DOS) or 12 (under Windows)

Same explanation as for (a) above applies to this program.

(c)   #include <iostream.h>

```
class base
{
    protected :

        int i ;
```

```
    public :

        base( )
        {
            cout << endl << &i ;
        }
} ;

class derived : public base
{
    public :

        derived( ) : base( )
        {
            cout << endl << &i ;
        }
} ;

void main( )
{
    derived d1 ;
    base b1 ;
}
```

Ans

The output would be:

```
0x8f9c0ffe
0x8f9c0ffe
0x8f9c0ffc
```

When we create an object of the derived class it is always the base class constructor that gets executed before the derived class constructor. But the control always goes to the derived class constructor for the information about which base class

constructor should be called. Hence when the object *d1* is
created the constructor of the class *derived* gets called. The
derived( ) : base( ) first calls base class's zero-argument
constructor. This prints the address of the *protected* data
member *i* of the base class. Then the derived class's
constructor gets executed which again prints the address of *i*.
Next, an object *b1* of base class is created which calls the
constructor of the *base* class and the address of *i* gets printed.

(d)   ```cpp
#include <iostream.h>
class base
{
    protected :

        int i ;

    public :

        void funct( )
        {
            cout << endl << &i ;
        }
} ;

class derived : public base
{
    private :

        int i ;

    public :

        derived( )
        {
            cout << endl << &i ;
            funct( ) ;
        }
```
```

```
};

void main( )
{
    derived d1 ;
}
```

Ans

The output would be:

```
0x8f990ffe
0x8f990ffc
```

When the object *d1* gets created, the *cout* statement in the constructor prints the address of the data member *i* of class *derived*. Then the function *funct( )* of base class is called which prints the address of the data member *i* of the class *base*.

(e)
```
#include <iostream.h>
int top = 3 ;

class base
{
    protected :

        int top ;

    public :

        base( )
        {
            top = 2 ;
            cout << endl << top ;
        }
```

```
};

class derived : public base
{
    private :

        int  top ;

    public :

        derived( ) : base( )
        {
            top = 1 ;
            cout << endl << top ;
            cout << endl << base::top ;
            cout << endl << ::top ;
        }
};

void main( )
{
    derived  d1 ;
}
```

Ans

The output would be:

2
1
2
3

When the object *d1* is created, the constructor of the class *base* gets called which prints the value of the data member *top*, which is 2. Then the *derived* class's constructor gets executed it prints the value of data member *top* declared in the derived class, which is 1. The *base::top* refers to the data member *top* of the class *base* and hence prints 2. Finally value of the global variable *top* gets printed which is 3.

(f)
```cpp
#include <iostream.h>
class index
{
    protected :

        int  count ;

    public :

        index( )
        {
            count = 0 ;
        }

        void operator ++( )
        {
            count++ ;
        }
        void display( )
        {
            cout << endl << count ;
        }
} ;

void main( )
{
    index  c ;
    c++ ;
    c.display( ) ;
    ++c ;
    c.display( ) ;
}
```

Ans

The output would be:

1
2

The same overloaded *operator ++( )* gets called for both the pre and post-incrementation ++ operators.

(g)
```
#include <iostream.h>
class base
{
    public :

        base( )
        {
            cout << endl << "third" ;
        }
};

class derived1 : public base
{
    public :

        derived1( ) : base( )
        {
            cout << endl << "second" ;
        }
};

class derived2 : public derived1
{
    public :

        derived2( ) : derived1( )
        {
            cout << endl << "first" ;
```

```
        }
};

void main( )
{
    derived2 d ;
}
```

Ans

The output would be:

```
third
second
first
```

This is an example of multiple levels of inheritance that shows that in the inheritance hierarchy the constructors get executed from base to derived.

Q 7.5

Point out the errors, if any, in the following programs.

(a)
```
class base1
{
    int b1 ;
};

class base2
{
    int b2 ;
};

class derived : public base1, base2
{
};

void main( )
```

```
{
}
```

Ans

No Error.

(b)
```cpp
#include <iostream.h>
void print( ) ;

class base1
{
    protected :

        void print( )
        {
            cout << "Hello" ;
        }
} ;

class base2
{
    public :

        void print ( )
        {
            cout << "Hi" ;
            ::print( ) ;
        }
} ;

void print( )
{
    cout << "err" ;
}

void main( )
```

```
{
    base1 b1 ;
    base2 b2 ;
    b1.print( ) ;
    b2.print( ) ;
}
```

Ans

Error. The *protected* member function *print( )* cannot be accessed from *main( )*.

(c)
```
#include <iostream.h>
class base
{
    private :

        int i ;

    public ·

        float j ;
        base( )
        ʃ
            i = j = 99 ;
        }
};

class derived : public base
{
    public :

        derived( ) : base( )
        {
            cout << i << j ;
        }
};
```

```
void main( )
{
    derived d1 ;
}
```

Ans

Error. The *private* data member *i* of the *base* class cannot be accessed in the *derived* class.

(d)   #include <iostream.h>

```
class base
{
    protected :

            int i ;
            float j ;

    public :

            base( )
            {
                i = j = 99 ;
            }
};

class derived : public base
{
    public :

            derived( ) : base( )
            {
                cout << i << j ;
            }
};

void main( )
```

```
{
    derived  d1 ;
}
```

Ans

No Error.

(e)
```
#include <iostream.h>
class base
{
    public :

        void f1( )
        {
            cout << "cout" ;
        }
} ;

class derived : public base
{
    public :

        void f2( )
        {
            cout << "cin" ;
        }
} ;

void main( )
{
    base  b1 ;
    derived  d1 ;
    b1.f2( ) ;
    d1.f1( ) ;
}
```

Ans

Error. *f2( )* is not a member function of the class *base*.

(f)   ```cpp
#include <iostream.h>
class base
{
    public :

        void func1( )
        {
            cout << "Hello" ;
        }
};

class der1 : public base
{
    public :

        void func2( )
        {
            cout << endl << "Hi" ;
        }
};

class der2 : private base
{
    public :

        void func3( )
        {
            cout << endl << "Goodbye!" ;
        }
};

void main( )
{
    der1 o1 ;
```
```

```
    der2  o2 ;
    o1.func1( ) ;
    o2.func1( ) ;
}
```

Ans

Error. Since the class *der2* is derived *privately* from the class *base*, the *public* members of the class *base* become *private* members for the class *der2*. Hence function *func1( )* cannot be accessed through object *o2*.

(g)
```
#include <iostream.h>

class base
{
    public :

        base( )
        {
            cout << "base class" ;
        }
} ;

class derived : public base
{
    public :

        void a( ) : base( )
        {
            cout << "derived class" ;
        }
} ;

void main( )
{
    derived  d ;
}
```

Ans

Error. In this program *a( )* is a member function of the class. The convention *void a( ) : base( )* is applicable to the constructors and not to the member functions.

Q 7.6

Suppose there is a base class *B* and a derived class *D* derived from *B*. *B* has two *public* member functions *b1( )* and *b2( )*, whereas *D* has two member functions *d1( )* and *d2( )*. Write these classes for the following different situations:

(a) *b1( )* should be accessible in *main( )*, *b2( )* should not be.

(b) Neither *b1( )*, nor *b2( )* should be accessible in *main( )*.

(c) Both *b1( )* and *b2( )* should be accessible in *main( )*.

Taking into consideration that the functions are called using the object of class *D*.

Ans

Case (a) :

b1( ) should be accessible in *main( )*, *b2( )* should not be.

```
class B
{
    public :

        void b1( )
        {
        }

        void b2( )
        {
        }
```

```
};

class D : public B
{
    private :

        B::b2 ;

    public :

        void d1( )
        {
        }

        void d2( )
        {
        }
};
```

or

```
class B
{
    public :

        void b1( )
        {
        }

        void b2( )
        {
        }
};

class D : private B
{
    public :

        B::b1 ;
```

```
        void d1( )
        {
        }

        void d2( )
        {
        }
};
```

Case (b) :

Neither *b1( )*, nor *b2( )* should be accessible in *main( )*.

```
class B
{
    public :

        void b1( )
        {
        }

        void b2( )
        {
        }
};

class D : private B
{
    public :

        void d1( )
        {
        }

        void d2( )
        {
        }
```

```
};
```

Case (c) :

Both *b1( )* and *b2( )* should be accessible in *main( )*.

```
class B
{
    public :

        void b1( )
        {
        }

        void b2( )
        {
        }
};

class D : public B
{
    public :

        void d1( )
        {
        }

        void d2( )
        {
        }
};
```

Q 7.7

If a class *D* is derived from two base classes *B1* and *B2*, then write these classes each containing a zero-argument constructor. Ensure that while building an object of type *D*, firstly the constructor of

B2 gets called followed by that of *B1*. Also provide a destructor in each class. In what order would these destructors get called?

Ans

```
class B1
{
    public :

            B1( )
            {
            }

            ~B1( )
            {
            }
};

class B2
{
    public :

            B2( )
            {
            }

            ~B2( )
            {
            }
};

class D : public B2, B1
{
    public :

            D( )
            {
            }
```

```
        ~D( )
        {
        }
};

void main( )
{
    D d;
}
```

The class *D* is derived from two classes *B1* and *B2*. When destructors are called then order of *B1* and *B2* mentioned in the declaration of the derived class matters. As the class has been declared as, *class D : public B2, B1,* when the object *d* gets destroyed firstly the destructor of the class *D* gets called then the destructor of the class *B1* followed by the destructor of the class *B2*.

Virtual Functions

Q 8.1

What are pure virtual functions?

Ans

A pure virtual function is a virtual function with the expression = 0 added to the declaration. This can be explained with the help of following example:

```
class base
{
    public :

        virtual void fun( ) = 0 ;
} ;
```

The function *fun( )* is known as pure virtual function.

Q 8.2

What is an abstract class?

Ans

A class that contains at least one pure virtual function is called an abstract class. An abstract class cannot be instantiated. We create such a class when a class is too general and it is irrelevant to create objects of such a class. For example, a class *shape*. But classes like *line*, *rectangle*, *circle*, etc. are specific classes and objects of these classes carry some meaning. Abstract classes are used mainly for polymorphic calls.

Q 8.3

Is it legal to create a pointer of an abstract base class?

Ans

Yes. Even though we cannot create an object of an abstract base class, it is perfectly valid to create a pointer of an abstract base class.

Q 8.4

What is static binding and dynamic binding?

Ans

The term binding refers to the connection between a function call and the actual code executed as a result of the call.

When a function call gets resolved at compile-time it is called static binding or early binding. When the call gets resolved at runtime it is called dynamic binding or late binding.

Q 8.5

What is a VTABLE?

Ans

A VTABLE contains addresses of virtual functions. The compiler creates a VTABLE for each class that contains virtual functions and for classes that are derived from it. The VTABLE contains the addresses in the order in which virtual functions are defined within the class.

Let us understand the VTABLE with the help of the following example:

```
class shape
{
   public :

      virtual void draw1( )
      {
      }

      virtual void draw2( )
      {
      }
};

class circle : public shape
{
   public :

      void draw1( )
      {
      }

      void draw2( )
      {
      }
};

void main( )
```

```
{
  shape *p, q ;
  circle c ;
  p = &q ;
  p -> draw2( ) ;
  p = &c ;
  p -> draw2( ) ;
}
```

Whenever we create an object of the class, the class gets loaded into the memory and the VTABLE gets created. In this program we have created an object of *shape* as well as of *circle*. Hence there will be two VTABLEs in memory. The in-memory view of the VTABLEs is shown in the following figure:

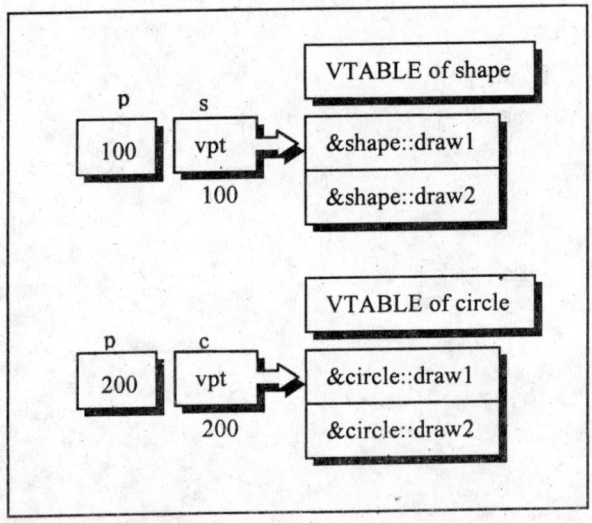

In our program when an object *c* of the class *circle* is created, the VTABLE of the *circle* class also gets created and its address gets stored in the first 2 bytes of the object.

When the compiler encounters a call,

p -> draw2( ) ;

it generates the code to extract first two bytes of the object whose address is stored in the pointer *p*. Before a call to *draw2( )* we have assigned an address of *q* to *p*. Hence first two bytes of *q* would be extracted. This gives the address of the VTABLE. The compiler also adds a number to this address. This number is actually an offset in the VTABLE. Since we have called *draw2( )*, 2 would be added to the address of VTABLE. This is because there are two functions in the class, *draw1( )* and *draw2( )*. According to the order of their definition the address of *draw1( )* would be stored in the first 2 bytes of the VTABLE, whereas, the address of *draw2( )* would be stored in the next 2 bytes.

The figure shows that there are two VTABLES: one for the base class *shape* and another for derived class *circle*. There are two virtual functions *draw1( )* and *draw2( )* in the base class *shape*. We have overridden these two virtual functions in the derived class.

Note that in the above explanation wherever we have stated 2 bytes, under Windows it should be treated as 4 bytes.

Q 8.6

What is VPTR?

Ans

The address of the VTABLE stored in the object is known as VPTR.

Q 8.7

What is upcasting?

Ans

Upcasting means storing the address of the derived class object in the base class pointer.

Q 8.8

What is a virtual destructor?

Ans

Refer Q 8.18 (u).

Q 8.9

What is the ideal place for defining a constructor and why?

Ans

Any function or constructor that is defined inside the class is by default inline. Usually we define the constructor inside the class believing that by using *inlining* we would be able to avoid the overheads involved in calling a constructor. But consider what all is done inside the constructor:

- When an object containing virtual functions is created, the constructor initializes the VPTR to point to the proper VTABLE. The compiler secretly inserts the VPTR initialization code into the constructor (if you have virtual functions).
- The constructor also calls the base class constructor.
- The constructor initializes the part of the object specific to the current class.

As a result, the size of the constructor grows to a limit where the savings we get from reduced function-call overheads are nullified. If we make a lot of inline constructor calls, our code size can grow without any benefits in speed. Because of the convenience of writing tiny constructors as *inline* we may still be tempted to keep them *inline*. But when we're looking for improving efficiency of our code, remember we have to remove *inline* constructors and define them outside the class.

Q 8.10

What are virtual base classes? When should they be used?

Ans

Consider the situation where there is one parent class called *base* and two classes derived from it, *derived1* and *derived2*. Suppose we derive a class *derived3* from *derived1* and *derived2*. Now suppose a member function of *derived3* class wants to access data or functions in the *base* class. Since *derived1* and *derived2* are derived from *base*, each inherits a copy of *base*. This copy is referred to as a *subobject*. Each subobject contains its own copy of *base*'s data. This is shown in the following figure.

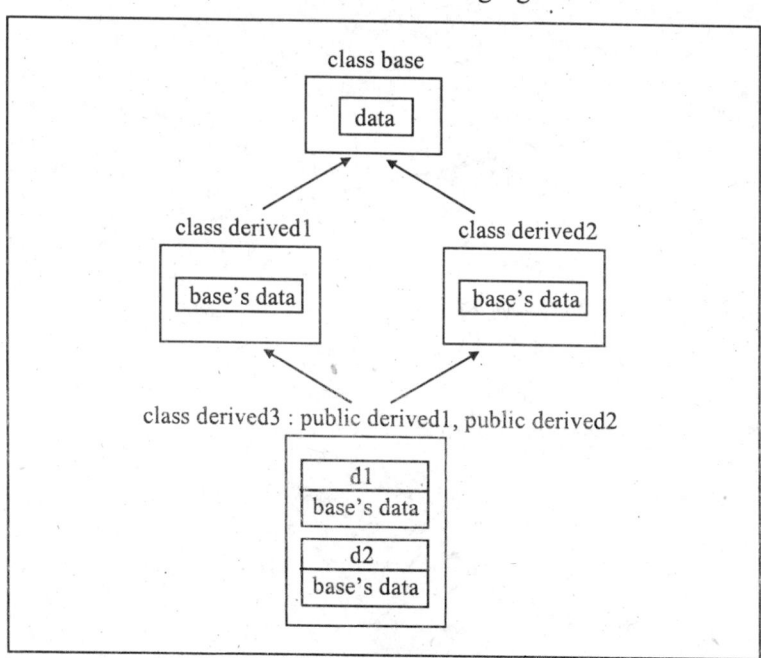

Now when *derived3* refers to the data in the *base* class, which of the two copies will it access? This is an ambiguous situation for the compiler, hence it reports an error. To get rid of this ambiguity, we should make *derived1* and *derived2* as *virtual* base classes as shown in the following program.

```cpp
#include <iostream.h>

class base
{
    protected :

        int  data ;

    public :

        base( )
        {
            data = 500 ;
        }
} ;

class derived1 : virtual public base
{
} ;

class derived2 : virtual public base
{
} ;

class derived3 : public derived1, public derived2
{
    public :

        int getdata( )
        {
            return  data ;
        }
```

```
};

void main( )
{
    derived3 ch ;
    int a ;

    a = ch.getdata( ) ;
    cout << a ;
}
```

Using the keyword *virtual* in the two base classes causes them to share the single subobject of the *base* class, which eliminates the ambiguity. Since there is only one subobject there is no ambiguity when it is referred in the *derived3* class. Here *derived1* and *derived2* are known as *virtual base classes*.

The ambiguity that we discussed occurs not only in the case of member data but also in case of member functions.

Q 8.11

Why member functions are not *virtual* by default?

Ans

The mechanism of virtual functions is not very efficient. As compared to a simple CALL to an absolute address, there are more sophisticated assembly instructions required to set up the *virtual* function call. This requires both code space and execution time. All non-*virtual* function calls are implemented through early binding and all *virtual* function calls are implemented through late binding. Thus, had all function calls in C++ been implemented through late binding, the efficiency would have suffered heavily.

Hence the *virtual* function is an option, and by default the language uses the non-virtual mechanism which is of course faster. In short, if you don't use it, you don't pay for it.

Q 8.12

Why destructors are not *virtual* by default?

Ans

Suppose a class *der* is derived from a class *base*. If we now create a *der* class object by saying

```
base *p ;
p = new der ;
```

then firstly the *base* class constructor would be called followed by a call to the *der* class constructor. If we now say *delete p* then destruction should proceed from *der* to *base*. This can be ensured by declaring the *base* class destructor as virtual. When we declare virtual destructor, time is spent in building the VTABLE. If we do not intend to create objects through *new* then there is no need for base class destructor to be *virtual*. Hence there is no need to create a VTABLE. Had destructors been *virtual* by default then unnecessarily time would have been spent for building VTABLE even if you don't need it. Hence destructors are not made *virtual* by default.

Q 8.13

What is object slicing?

Ans

If an object of a derived class is assigned to a base class object, the compiler accepts it, but it copies only the base portion of the object. It slices off the derived portion of the object. Because of this, upcasting into an object is seldom done. This is shown in the following example:

```
#include <iostream.h>

class base
{
    private :

        int i, j ;
};

class derived : public base
{
    private :

        int k ;
};

void main( )
{
    base b ;
    derived d ;

    b = d ;
}
```

Here b contains i and j whereas, d contains i, j and k. On assignment only i and j of d get copied into i and j of b. k doesn't get copied. In effect object d got sliced.

Q 8.14

Can we declare a static function as virtual?

Ans

No. The virtual function mechanism is used on the specific object that determines which virtual function to call. Since the *static* functions are not any way related to objects, they cannot be declared as *virtual*.

Q 8.15

Is it necessary that the virtual function overridden in the derived class must have the same signature?

Ans

Yes. If a virtual function of a base class is overridden in the derived class with different return type or different parameter types then it becomes a totally new function of the derived class.

Q 8.16

Is it compulsory to override a virtual function?

Ans

No. If we do not override the virtual function in the derived class then the VTABLE of the derived class would contain the address of the base class virtual function.

Q 8.17

Can we redefine a virtual function of the base class as a non-virtual function in the derived class?

Ans

No. The virtual function can be overridden in the derived class but cannot be made non-virtual.

Q 8.18

State whether the following statements are True or False:

(a) Virtual functions implement one form of polymorphism.

Ans

True. In class hierarchy, the virtual functions permit functions from different classes to be executed through the same function call. These functions have the same name but their definitions are different.

(b) Virtual functions permit calling of derived class functions using a base class pointer.

Ans

True. This can be explained with the help of following example:

```cpp
#include <iostream.h>
class base
{
    public :

        virtual void fun( )
        {
            cout << " In base : fun " << endl ;
        }
};

class der : public base
{
    public :

        void fun( )
        {
            cout << " In der : fun " << endl ;
        }
};

void main( )
{
    base *b ;
    der  d ;
    b = &d ;
    b -> fun( ) ;
```

}

The output would be:

In der fun( )

From the output it is clear that the derived class's *fun( )* function is getting called.

(c) Each object has its own VTABLE.

Ans

False. The VTABLE belongs to a class. All objects of the class share the same VTABLE. The objects contain the address of the VTABLE in their first 2 bytes (under DOS) or in first 4 bytes (under Windows).

(d) There is only one VTABLE per class.

Ans

True.

(e) We can access the VTABLE using the *this* pointer.

Ans

True. This is shown in the following example:

```
#include <iostream.h>

class sample
{
    public :

        virtual void _cdecl fun ( int  q )
        {
            cout << "fun " << q ;
```

```
            }

        void g( )
        {
            int *p = ( int * ) this ; // address of the object

            p = ( int * ) *p ; // address of the VTABLE
            p = ( int * ) *p ; // address of the 1st virtual function

            void ( _cdecl *pfun ) ( sample * const, int ) ;
            pfun = ( void ( _cdecl * ) ( sample * const, int ) ) p ;
            ( *pfun ) ( this, 25 ) ;
        }
};

void main( )
{
    sample s ;
    s.g( ) ;
}
```

In this program *fun( )* is a virtual function. Hence when an object of this class would be created the class would get loaded in memory. Also, the VTABLE of this class would be created and its address would be stored in the first two bytes of the object.

When the function *g( )* is called from *main( )* using the object *s*, the *this* pointer in the *g( )* function would get filled with the address of s.

We have typecast the address of the object (stored in *this* pointer) into an *int* pointer using the statement *int *p = (int *) this*. This is because we want to extract the first two bytes of the object, since they contain the address of the VTABLE. To extract the address we have written the statement, *p = (int *) *p*. Now *p* would contain the address of VTABLE. To obtain the address of the first virtual function in the VTABLE we need to extract its address from the VTABLE. Since *fun( )* is the first virtual function its address would be in the first two bytes of the VTABLE. Hence we have extracted the address of the first two bytes by writing the statement, *p = (int *) *p*.

Now *p* contains the address of the first virtual function, which is *fun( )* in our case. To call the function we have to store the current value of *p* in a pointer to function *pfun*, which is declared as

void (_cdecl *pfun) (sample * const, int) ;

Here *void* is the return type of the function *fun( )*. *_cdecl* is a calling convention and *sample *const, int* are the arguments passed to the function. The first argument passed as *sample * const* is hidden (which is the *this* pointer) and hence is not shown in the function definition.

(f) *this* pointer and VPTR are same.

Ans

False. There is no such keyword as VPTR. The address in the object that points to the VTABLE is called *vpointer* and VPTR is its abbreviation. Since the *this* pointer points to an object it is not same as the VPTR.

(g) There is one VPTR per VTABLE.

Ans

False. This is because each object contains a VPTR in it.

(h) There is one VPTR per object.

Ans

True. But all the objects have the same VPTR.

(i) The VPTR always points to the VTABLE of the class.

Ans

True.

(j) Virtual functions permit functions from different classes to be executed through the same function call.

Ans

True. This is one form of polymorphism.

(k) Pure virtual function can never have a body.

Ans

False. If the pure virtual function has a body then we can call this function from the derived class overridden function. This is shown in the following example:

```cpp
#include <iostream.h>

class base
{
    public :

        virtual void fun( ) = 0
        {
            cout << "base fun" << endl ;
        }
};

class derived : public base
{
    public :

        void fun( )
        {
```

```
            cout << "derived fun" << endl ;
            base::fun( ) ;
        }
    };

    void main( )
    {
        derived d ;
        d.fun( ) ;
    }
```

(l) Pure virtual constructors can have a body.

Ans

False. There is no such entity as pure virtual constructor. Even if we were allowed to declare a pure virtual constructor we would not be able to override it.

(m) We can never build an object from a class containing a pure virtual function.

Ans

True. If the class contains a pure virtual function then that class is abstract. If someone creates an object of such a class and calls the function having no body it would result in an error. Hence the object of such a class cannot be created.

Also, by creating a pure virtual function we can force the derived classes to override this function to be able to create the objects of the derived classes. This technique is helpful in program design.

(n) A class containing a pure virtual function is called an abstract base class.

Ans

True.

(o) Virtual function calls work faster than normal function calls.

Ans

False. This is because the call to the virtual function is resolved at runtime. Moreover the call is resolved after retrieving the address of the function from the VTABLE. This consumes time.

The call to the normal function is resolved at compile time. Also there is no mechanism of VTABLE involved in calling the normal function.

(p) In a class hierarchy of several levels, if we want a function at any level to be called through a base class pointer, then the function must be declared as *virtual* in the base class.

Ans

True.

(q) Virtual functions can be safely invoked using objects.

Ans

True.

(r) The behaviour of virtual functions is same irrespective of whether we invoke them through pointers or references.

Ans

True.

(s) While building an object it doesn't matter whether the base class constructor is called first or the derived class constructor is called first.

Ans

False. It matters when the designer of the derived class wants to initialize the data members of the base class in the constructor of the derived class. At such a time if the base class constructor is called after the derived class constructor, then the base class constructor may reinitialize the data members resulting into having no effect of initialization in the derived class. Construction of an object must proceed from base towards derived.

(t) While destroying an object firstly the derived class destructor should be called followed by the base class destructor.

Ans

True. This can be explained with the help of the following example:

```
class base
{
    public :

        int *p ;

        base( )
        {
            p = new int [ 10 ] ;
        }

        ~base( )
        {
            delete [ ] p ;
        }
};
```

```
class derived : public base
{
    public .

        void add ( int  i )
        {
            // add int in an array
        }

        ~derived( )
        {
            // dump the array elements in file
        }
};

void main( )
{
    derived  d ;
    d.add ( 10 ) ;
}
```

When the object of the class *derived* is created, *base* class constructor gets called which allocates memory for 10 integer elements. Then the function *add( )* is called which adds an integer element to the array. Finally when the object *d* is destroyed the code inside the destructor of the *derived* class stores the array elements in the file. Then the destructor of the *base* class is called which deallocates the memory.

If the destructor of the base class is called before the derived class destructor, then the memory would be deallocated and we would not be able to write the array elements in the file.

(u) A virtual destructor ensures a proper calling order for the destructors in the class hierarchy.

Ans

True. This can be explained with the help of following example:

```
class base
{
    public :

            virtual ~base( )
            {
            }
};

class derived : public base
{
            int *p ;

    public :

            derived( )
            {
                p = new int ;
            }

            ~derived( )
            {
                delete p ;
            }
};

void main( )
{
    base *b = new derived ;
    delete b ;
}
```

In *main( )* when the object of class *derived* is created using *new*, its constructor gets called. The memory is allocated for an *int* in the constructor. The address returned by *new* is stored in the pointer to the *base* class, *b*. When *delete* is called on *b*, the destructor of only the *base* class would get called if it were not declared as *virtual*. Hence *delete p* would not be executed.

When we make the *base* class destructor *virtual*, the *derived class* destructor gets called first and then the *base* class destructor gets called. Hence *delete p* does get executed.

(v) A pure virtual destructor can have a function body.

Ans

False. There is no such concept of pure virtual destructor in C++.

(w) The virtual function of a base class that is overridden in the derived class also becomes virtual.

Ans

True.

(x) An abstract class typically doesn't need a constructor.

Ans

True. Since we cannot instantiate an object from an abstract class there is no need of a constructor in that class.

Q 8.19

What will be the output of the following programs:

(a)
```
#include <iostream.h>
class base
```

```
{
    public :

        virtual void fun( )
        {
            cout << "fun of base" ;
        }

        void run( )
        {
            fun( ) ;
        }
} ;

class derived : public base
{
    public :

        void fun( )
        {
            cout << "fun of derived" ;
        }
} ;

void main( )
{
    derived  d ;
    d.run( ) ;
}
```

Ans

The output would be:

fun of derived

When the *run( )* function is called using *d*, the base class *run( )* gets called. From this function there is a call to the *fun( )* function. From *run( )* function the *fun( )* function is called. Since the *run( )* function is called through the object *d*, the *this* pointer contains the address of the object *d* in it. Being a virtual function, *fun( )* of that class gets called whose object's address is stored in the *this* pointer. Since the address of *d* is stored in the *this* pointer, the *fun( )* function of the *derived* class gets called.

For detailed explanation, refer Q 8.5.

(b)
```cpp
#include <iostream.h>
class base
{
    public :

        void fun( )
        {
            fun1( ) ;
        }

        void fun1( )
        {
            cout << "fun1 of base" ;
        }
} ;

class derived : public base
{
    public :

        void fun1( )
        {
            cout << "fun1 of derived" ;
        }
} ;

void main( )
```

```
{
    derived d ;
    d.fun( ) ;
}
```

Ans

The output would be:

fun1 of base

When the function *fun( )* is called, *base* class's *fun( )* gets called, as it is not present in the *derived* class. From the function *fun( )* there is a call to *fun1( )*. This would call the *base* class *fun1( )*. This is because the *base* class *fun1( )* is a non-virtual function and hence the *fun1( )* of the same class would get called.

(c)
```
#include <iostream.h>
class base
{
    public :

        virtual void fun1( )
        {
            cout << endl << "In base::fun1" ;
        }
};

class derived1 : public base
{
    public :

        void fun1( )
        {
            cout << endl << "In derived::fun1" ;
        }
```

```
            virtual void fun2( )
            {
                cout << endl << "In derived1::fun2" ;
            }
};

class derived2 : public derived1
{
    public :

        void fun1( )
        {
            cout << endl << "In derived2::fun1" ;
        }

        void fun2( )
        {
            cout << endl << "In derived2::fun2" ;
        }
};

void main( )
{
    base  *ptr1 ;
    derived1  *ptr2 ;
    base  b ;
    derived2  d ;
    ptr1 = &b ;
    ptr2 = &d ;
    ptr1 -> fun1( ) ;
    ptr2 -> fun1( ) ;
    ( ( derived1 * ) ptr2 ) -> fun2( ) ;
}
```

Ans

The output would be:

```
In base::fun1
In derived2::fun1
In derived2::fun2
```

ptr1, which is pointer to *base* class object, is holding the address of the *base* class object *b*. So when the function *fun1( )* is called through *ptr1* it calls the function *fun1( )* of *base* class.

In the statement,

```
ptr2 = &d ;
```

the address of *derived2* class object gets stored in the pointer to the *derived1* class object. When the function *fun1( )* is called through *ptr2* it calls the function *fun1( )* of *derived2* class, because the function *fun1( )* is *virtual* in the *base* class (function *fun1( )* of *derived1* class automatically becomes *virtual*).

In the statement,

```
( ( derived1 * ) ptr2 ) -> fun2( ) ;
```

the pointer *ptr2* which is of the type *derived1 * is typecast into its own type *derived1 * , so there will be no effect of typecasting on it and hence the function *fun2( )* of the *derived2* class gets called.

(d)
```
#include <iostream.h>
class base
{
    public :

        virtual void fun( )
        {
            cout << endl << "In base::fun( )" ;
        }
};
```

```cpp
class derived1 : virtual public base
{
    public :

        void fun( )
        {
            cout << endl << "In derived1::fun( )" ;
        }
} ;

class derived2 : virtual public base
{
    public :

        void fun( )
        {
            cout << endl << "In derived2::fun( )" ;
        }
} ;

class derived3 : public derived1, public derived2
{
    public :

        void fun( )
        {
            cout << endl << "In derived3::fun( )" ;
            derived1::fun( ) ;
        }
} ;

void main( )
{
    base *b ;

    derived1  d1 ;
    b = &d1 ;
    b -> fun( ) ;
```

```
        derived2 d2 ;
        b = &d2 ;
        b -> fun( ) ;

        derived3 d3 ;
        b = &d3 ;
        b -> fun( ) ;
}
```

Ans

```
In derived1::fun( )
In derived2::fun( )
In derived3::fun( )
In derived1::fun( )
```

The pointer *b* is of type *base* *, which initially holds the address of the object *d1* of type *derived1*. The statement *b -> fun( )* calls the overridden function *fun( )* of class *derived1* which prints the statement "In derived1::fun( )".

Then the pointer *b* is made to point to object *d2* of type *derived2*. Now the statement *b -> fun( )* calls the function *fun( )* of class *derived2* which prints the statement "In derived2::fun( )".

Finally the pointer *b* is made to point to object *d3* of type *derived3*. Now the statement *b -> fun( )* calls the function *fun( )* of class *derived3* which prints the statement "In derived3::fun( )". Next it calls the function *fun( )* of the class *derived1* which prints the statement "In derived1::fun( )".

Q 8.20

Point out the error if any in the following program:

```
#include <iostream.h>

class base
{
```

```
    public :

        virtual void fun1( ) = 0 ;

        void fun2( )
        {
            cout << "in fun2" ;
        }
};

class derived : public base
{
    public :

        void fun3( )
        {
            cout << "in fun3" ;
        }
};

void main( )
{
    derived  d ;
    d.fun3( ) ;
}
```

Ans

Error would occur in creating the object *d* of the class *derived*. The function *fun1( )* is declared as pure virtual function in the class *base* and is not implemented in the *derived* class and hence *derived* class becomes an abstract class, and we cannot create objects from an abstract class.

Q 8.21

Write a program that contains a class *derived*, derived from *base*. The *base* class should have a virtual function *fun( )* and it should be overridden in *derived*. Try to call *fun( )* from the constructor of the base class and watch the results.

Ans

The program is as follows:

```cpp
#include <iostream.h>

class base
{
    public :

        base( )
        {
            fun( ) ;
        }

        virtual void fun( )
        {
            cout << "fun of base" ;
        }
} ;

class derived : public base
{
    public :

        void fun( )
        {
            cout << "fun of derived" ;
        }
} ;

void main( )
{
    derived  d ;
}
```

Ans

The output would be:

fun of base

During the creation of the object *d* of type *derived*, the constructor of the class *base* is called first. From the constructor the virtual function *fun( )* is being called. Being a virtual function, ideally the derived class's *fun( )* should have been called. Since at this stage only the base class part of the object has been constructed (derived class parts has not been constructed so far since the derived class constructor is yet to get called), base class's *fun( )* gets called. Thus the virtual function mechanism doesn't work within the constructor.

Input/Output In C++

Q 9.1

What is a stream?

Ans

Stream is a general name given to the flow of data. To represent different kinds of data different streams are used. For example, the standard output stream flows to the screen display, the standard input stream flows from the keyboard. In C++, a stream is represented by an object of a particular class.

Q 9.2

What are the disadvantages of using *printf( )/scanf( )* functions?

Ans

There are 5 major disadvantages of *printf( )/scanf( )*. They are as follows:

– Remembering all the format specifiers in *printf( )/scanf( )* is not an easy job.

- *printf( )/scanf( )* do not carry out conversions logically. For example, 3.5 printed using *%d* neither produces 3 nor 4.
- In case of a mismatch between the specifiers and the type to be printed/scanned, the *printf( )/scanf( )* functions do not report any warning.
- We cannot extend *printf( )* to accommodate new data types. Thus the primary goal of C++, the ability to add new data types with ease, gets defeated.
- *printf( )/scanf( )* are variable-argument list functions. An interpreter is loaded for such functions at runtime. This increases overheads, because, even if we print only a character, logic that prints out *long*, *double*, etc. still gets loaded. This leads to wastage of memory space.

Q 9.3

What are the three parts of an *iostream* system?

Ans

The three parts of an *iostream* system are as follows:

- A buffer, which acts as an intermediary between the generalized input-output system and some particular source or sink for characters. This has been implemented in the *streambuf* class.
- A specification system responsible for reporting errors and controlling formats. This has been implemented in the *ios* class.
- A translation system that converts C++ language's typed objects to a sequence of characters or vice versa. This has been implemented in classes like *istream*, *ostream*, *iostream*, etc.

Q 9.4

What is *ios*?

Ans

The I/O specification class (*ios*) is at the root of the *iostream* class hierarchy, as shown in the figure of the next question. This class contains features that are common to all streams. It includes flags for formatting the stream, error-status flags and the flags for file operation mode. It also includes a pointer to the *streambuf* class, which contains the actual memory buffer into which data is read or written, and the routines to handle its data. The classes derived from this class are used to input and output data.

Q 9.5

What are formatting flags in *ios* class?

Ans

The *ios* class contains formatting flags that help users to format the stream data. Formatting flags are a set of *enum* definitions. There are two types of formatting flags:

– On/Off flags
– Flags that work in group

The On/Off flags are turned on using the *setf( )* function and are turned off using the *unsetf( )* function. To set the on/off flags, the one argument *setf( )* function is used. The flags working in groups are set through the two-argument *setf( )* function.

For example, to left justify a string we can set the flag as,

```
cout.setf ( ios::left ) ;
cout << "KICIT Nagpur" ;
```

To remove the left justification for subsequent output we can say,

```
cout.unsetf ( ios::left ) ;
```

The flags that can be set/unset include *skipws*, *showbase*, *showpoint*, *uppercase*, *showpos*, *unitbuf* and *stdio*.

The flags that work in a group can have only one of these flags set at a time. To set these flags the second form of *setf( )* function is used, as discussed in the next question.

Q 9.6

What is the purpose of *ios::basefield* in the following statement?

cout.setf (ios::hex, ios::basefield) ;

Ans

This is an example of formatting flags that work in a group. There is a flag for each numbering system (base) like decimal, octal and hexadecimal. Collectively, these flags are referred to as *basefield* and are specified by *ios::basefield* flag. We can have only one of these flags on at a time. If we set the *hex* flag as *setf (ios::hex)* then we will set the *hex* bit but we won't clear the *dec* bit resulting in undefined behavior. The solution is to call *setf( )* as *setf (ios::hex, ios::basefield)*. This call first clears all the bits and then sets the *hex* bit.

Q 9.7

Why is *ios::* necessary in the following statement:

cout << setiosflags (ios::showbase) ;

Ans

showbase is the *enum* element defined within the class *ios*. Hence it can be accessed directly using the class name. Following example shows how the *enum* elements are directly accessed using the class name.

#include <iostream.h>

ss sample

```
    public :

        enum { first, second, third } ;
} ;

void main( )
{
    cout << sample::second ;
}
```

Q 9.8

Can we get the value of *ios* format flags?

Ans

Yes. The *ios::flags( )* member function gives the value of format flags. This function takes no arguments and returns a *long (typedef*ed *to fmtflags)* that contains the current format flags.

Q 9.9

Name the function that can skip certain number of characters present in the input stream?

Ans

The function is *cin::ignore( )*. The prototype of the function is as follows:

```
istream& ignore ( int n = 1, int d = EOF ) ;
```

Sometimes it happens that some extra characters are left in the input stream while taking the input such as, the '\n' (Enter) character. This extra character is then passed to the next input and may pose problem.

To get rid of such extra characters the *cin::ignore( )* function is used. This is equivalent to *fflush (stdin)* used in C Language. Thi function ignores the first *n* characters (if present) in the input stream, stops if delimiter *d* is encountered.

Q 9.10

Draw a chart showing hierarchy of various classes in the *iostream* library.

Ans

The following figure shows the hierarchy of various classes:

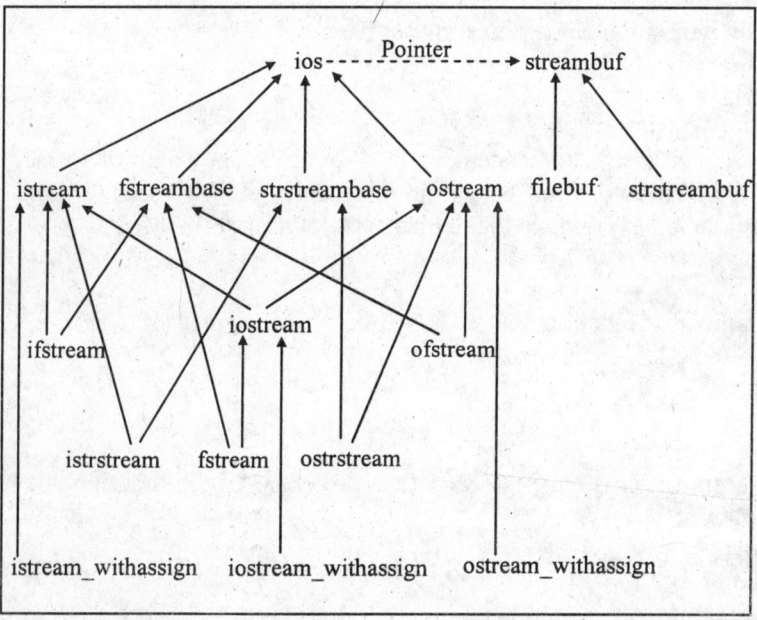

9.11

at does the *skipws* flag accomplish when used with *cin*?

Ans

While inputting the numbers through *cin* the whitespace characters such as '\n' and tab are ignored, as by default the *skipws* flag is set. In situations where we don't want whitespaces to be ignored, the *skipws* flag should be put off by using,

cin.unsetf (ios::skipws) ;

Q 9.12

When the *unitbuf* flag is used?

Ans

The unit buffering (*unitbuf*) flag should be turned on when we want to ensure that each character is output as soon as it is inserted into an output stream The same can be done using unbuffered output but unit buffering provides a better performance than the unbuffered output.

Q 9.13

What are error-status flags in *ios* class?

Ans

The error status flags are the enumerated data and are provided to report errors that occur in input and output operations like opening file, reading from file, writing to a file, reaching end of file, etc. For a detailed explanation refer Q 9.25.

Q 9.14

What are manipulators?

Ans

Manipulators are the instructions to the output stream to modify the output in various ways.

The manipulators provide a clean and easy way for formatted output in comparison to the formatting flags of the *ios* class. When manipulators are used, the formatting instructions are inserted directly into the stream.

Manipulators are of two types, those that take an argument and those that don't.

Q 9.15

What is *endl* and how it works?

Ans

endl is simply a function that takes as its argument an *ostream* reference. The declaration for *endl( )* in 'iostream.h' looks like this.

```
ostream& endl ( ostream& ) ;
```

Consider the statement

```
cout << endl ;
```

Since << is an overloaded operator, internally this statement becomes,

```
cout.operator << ( endl ) ;
```

endl( ) being a function, what is being passed to the overloaded operator is a pointer to a function. The << operator has been defined in 'iostream.h' as follows:

```
ostream & ostream::operator << ( ostream & ( *pfun ) (ostream & ) )
{
    return ( *pfun )( *this ) ;
}
```

This indicates that when we pass the address of *endl( )* to this function, it collects it in a pointer to a function that receives an *ostream* reference and returns an *ostream* reference. If you observe carefully, this matches the prototype of the *endl( )* function. Since this operator function is called through the *cout* object, the *this* pointer contains the address of *cout*. Hence **this* yields the object. This object is then passed to the *endl( )* function through the statement.

(*pfun)(*this) ;

On getting called all that the *endl( )* function does is emit a '\n' to the output stream.

Q 9.16

What is the difference between the manipulator and *setf( )* function?

Ans

The difference between the manipulator and *setf( )* function are as follows:

- The *setf( )* function is used to set the flags of the *ios* but manipulators directly inserts the formatting instructions into the stream.
- We can create user-defined manipulators but *setf( )* function uses data members of *ios* class only.
- The flags put on through the *setf( )* function can be put off through *unsetf( )* function. Such flexibility is not available with manipulators.

Q 9.17

What is the purpose of *istream* class?

Ans

The *istream* class performs activities specific to input. It is derived from the *ios* class. The most commonly used member function of this class is the overloaded >> operator which can extract values of all basic types. We can extract even a string using this operator.

This class contains a few miscellaneous functions; these functions and their purpose are shown in the following table:

Function	Purpose
putback (ch)	Inserts last character read, back into input stream
peek (ch)	Reads one character, leaves it in stream
num = gcount( )	Returns number of character read by a (immediately preceding) call to *get( )*, *getline( )*, or *read( )*
ignore (MAX, DELIM)	Extracts and discards up to MAX characters until (and including) the specified delimiter (typically '\n')

Q 9.18

What is an o*stream* class?

Ans

The *ostream* class handles output or insertion activities. This class is derived from *ios* class. The most commonly used member function of this class is the overloaded << operator function. Two more useful functions of this class are *put( )* and *flush( )*. The *put( )* function is used to put a character in the stream, whereas, *flush( )* function flushes the buffer and inserts a newline.

Q 9.19

What is an *iostream* class?

Ans

The *iostream* class is derived from both *istream* and *ostream* by multiple inheritance. It acts only as a base class from which other classes can be derived. Other than the constructors and destructors, it doesn't contain any other member functions. The classes derived from *iostream* can perform both input and output.

Q 9.20

What are _withassign_ classes?

Ans

Refer Q 9.41 (h).

Q 9.21

What is the limitation of *cin* while taking input for character array?

Ans

Consider the following statement,

```
char str [ 5 ] ;
cin >> str ;
```

While entering the value for *str* if we enter more than 5 characters then there is no provision in *cin* to check the arrays bounds. If the array overflows, it may be dangerous. This can be avoided by using the *get( )* function. This is shown in the following program:

```
#include <iostream.h>

void main( )
{
    char str [ 5 ] ;

    cout << "Enter your name : " ;
    cin.get ( str, 5 ) ;
    cout << str ;
}
```

Here, if more than five characters are entered, *get( )* accepts only first five characters and rest of the characters are ignored.

There are several forms of this *get( )* functions. They are shown in the following table.

Function	Purpose
get (ch)	Extracts one character into *ch*
get (str, MAX)	Extracts up to MAX characters into *str*
get (str, DELIM)	Extracts characters into array *str* until specified delimiter (typically '\n'). Leaves delimiting character in stream
get (str, MAX, DELIM)	Extracts characters into array *str* until MAX characters or the DELIM character. Leaves delimiting character in stream
getline (str, MAX, DELIM)	Extract characters into array *str*, until MAX characters or the DELIM character. Extracts delimiting character.

Q 9.22

How can the following statement work for testing the end of file, if *infile* is an *ifstream* object:

while (infile) ;

Ans

When the statement,

while (infile) ;

gets executed the following statements get called

```
ios::operator void * ( )
{
    return fail( ) ? 0 : this ;
}
```

This is a conversion function that tries to convert an *ifstream* object into a *void* pointer. Within it, it calls a *ios::fail( )* function which looks like this:

```
int fail( )
{
```

```
        return state & ( failbit | badbit | hardfail ) ;
}
```

Here *state* is an *ios* class variable and what is being tested with bitwise & operator is the status of various error flags. If this function returns a non-zero value (meaning end of file is not reached) then the conversion function simply returns the address of the object (*this*), otherwise it returns a zero. It is this address or zero that is checked in the *while* loop. If zero is returned the control jumps out of the *while* loop.

Note that the address returned has no significance except to be tested for a zero or non-zero value.

Q 9.23

What do the *nocreate* and *noreplace* flag ensure when they are used for opening a file?

Ans

nocreate and *noreplace* are file opening modes. A bit in the *ios* class defines these modes. The flag *nocreate* ensures that the file must exist before opening it. On the other hand the flag *noreplace* ensures that while opening a file for output it does not get overwritten with new one unless *ate* or *app* is set. When the *app* flag is set then whatever we write gets appended to the existing file. When *ate* flag is set we can start reading or writing at the end of the existing file.

Q 9.24

What problem do you think would we face if the following code were executed twice:

```
file.seekg ( 0L, ios::beg ) ;
while ( file.read ( ( char * ) &p, sizeof ( p ) ) )
      cout << p.name << endl << p.age ;
```

How would you solve the problem?

Ans

When we execute these statements for the first time the first statement sets the *get* pointer at the beginning of the file stream. The *while* loop reads each record and displays it on the screen. As a result the *get* pointer now gets set at the end of file.

When we execute these statements for the second time we are unable to read the record from the file even if the get pointer is set to the beginning of the file. This is because when we reach the end of the file, the end-of-file bit in the *state* variable of the *ios* class gets set. This bit remains set even if we reposition the get pointer to the beginning of the file. Hence when we try to read the record for the second time, the end of file condition is still satisfied. Hence no reading takes place.

To rectify this situation, whenever we reach the end of file and still want to use the file we should call the *ios::clear( )*, in the manner shown in the following statement:

file.clear( ) ;

This statement sets the end-of-file bit to zero in the *state* variable.

Q 9.25

What is a *state* variable and how would you obtain the value of a *state* variable?

Ans

state variable is an *ios* class variable and it stores the status of various error flags. The bits of *state* variable signify the various error states. The position of these bits and their meaning is given in the following figure.

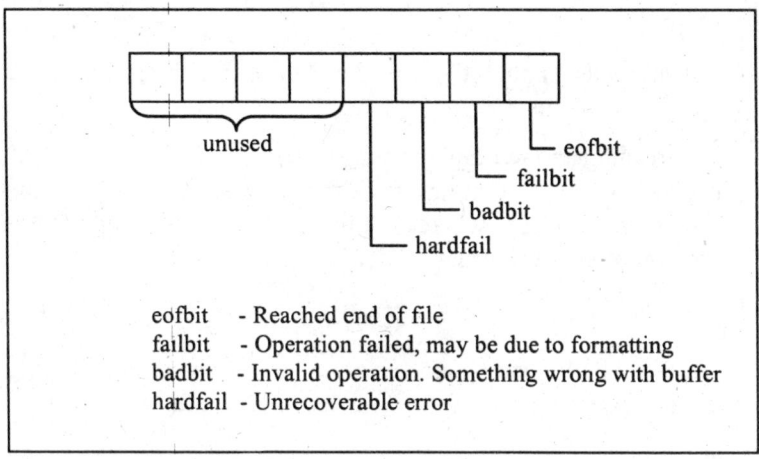

eofbit   - Reached end of file
failbit   - Operation failed, may be due to formatting
badbit   - Invalid operation. Something wrong with buffer
hardfail - Unrecoverable error

To get the value of *state* variable we need to call the function *ios::rdstate( )*. There are other functions like *eof( )*, *good( )*, *fail( )*, *hard( )* and *bad( )* that return the status of individual bits.

Q 9.26

Which are the three stream classes that are commonly used for disk I/O?

Ans

The stream classes that are used for disk I/O are shown with their purposes in the following table:

Class	Derived From	Purpose
ifstream	istream, fstreambase	Input from file
ofstream	ostream, fstreambase	Output to file
fstream	iostream, fstreambase	Both input and output

All these classes are declared in the file 'fstream.h'.

Q 9.27

In which mode should the file be opened for performing the following operations:

- both reading and writing in binary mode
- reading as well as writing, if the file does not exist a new one should get created, whereas if it is already existing then it should not get overwritten.

Ans

To perform both reading and writing in binary mode the file should be opened with the following open command:

```
fstream file ;
file.open ( filename, ios::in | ios::out | ios::binary ) ;
```

To perform reading as well as writing and to ensure that if the file does not exist a new one should get created, and if it already exists then it should not get overwritten, we need to open the file using the following open command:

```
fstream file ;
file.open ( filename, ios::in | ios::out | ios::noreplace ) ;
```

Q 9.28

What are different types of file opening modes?

Ans

There are several modes in which a stream object can be opened. Following table shows this:

Mode Bit	Result
in	Open for reading (default for *ifstream*)
out	Open for writing (default for *ofstream*)
ate	Start reading or writing at end of file (AT End)
app	Start writing at end of file (APPend)
trunc	Truncate file to zero length if it exists (TRUNCate)
norcreate	Error when opening if file does not already exist
noreplace	Error when opening for output if file already exists, unless *ate* or *app* is set
binary	Open file in binary (not text) mode

These bits can be combined using the logical OR operator.

Q 9.29

What is the difference between text mode and binary mode while performing file I/O operations?

Ans

The difference occurs while storing the number (integer or float). In text mode each digit in a number is stored as a character resulting in occupying more memory than necessary. For example, the float value 25.0979 will occupy 7 bytes in text mode but in the binary mode it occupies only 4 bytes.

So using text mode becomes inefficient while storing records that contain several numeric fields.

Q 9.30

What are *put* and *get* pointers?

Ans

These are the *long* integers associated with the streams. The value present in the *put* pointer specifies the byte number in the file from where next write would take place in the file. The *get* pointer specifies the byte number in the file from where the next reading should take place.

Q 9.31

What is the purpose of *seekp( )/seekg( )* function?

Ans

The *seekp( )* function positions the *put* pointer at the specific location in the file. The *seekp( )* function is overloaded to take either one or two parameters. If we use one-argument *seekp( )*, we can mention the position in bytes relative to the beginning of the file. In the two-argument version we can specify the position in bytes relative to the end of file, beginning of the file and current position. For this, we can use *end*, *beg* and *cur* flags respectively.

The *seekg( )* function works similar to *seekp( )* function but the major difference is that the first works on *get* pointer while the second works on *put* pointer.

Q 9.32

Which function gives you the current position of the file pointer?

Ans

We can get the current position of the file pointer by using the *tellp( )* member function of *ostream* class or *tellg( )* member function of *istream* class. These functions return (in bytes) positions of *put* pointer and *get* pointer respectively.

Q 9.33

Can we call *seekg( )* and *tellg( )* functions using *ofstream* object and *seekp( )* and *tellp( )* functions using *ifstream* object?

Ans

No. But if we use *fstream* for file I/O we can call both the sets of functions.

Q 9.34

Write the statement to position the file pointer at the beginning of the file using *seekg( )* function.

Ans

The statement,

```
file.seekg ( 0L, ios::beg ) ;
```

positions the file pointer at the beginning of the file.

Q 9.35

Would the following code work?

```
#include <iostream.h>

void main( )
{
    ostream o ;
    o << "Dream. Then make it happen! " ;
}
```

Ans

No. We cannot create the object of the *ostream* class because its constructor and copy constructor are declared *private*.

Q 9.36

If an error occurs while opening a file how can we check it?

Ans

This can be explained with the help of following code:

```cpp
#include <fstream.h>
#include <stdlib.h>

void main( )
{
    void check ( ofstream& ) ;

    ofstream file ;
    file.open ( "SAMPLE.TXT", ios::noreplace ) ;

    if ( ! file )
    {
        check ( file ) ;
        exit ( 1 ) ;
    }
    else
    {
        file << "Had cars been built like the OS," << endl
             << "we would have had more hospitals than homes" ;
        if ( ! file )
        {
            check ( file ) ;
            exit ( 2 ) ;
        }
    }
    file.close( ) ;
}

void check ( ofstream  &file )
{
    cout << endl << "Unable to open SAMPLE.TXT" ;
```

```
        cout << endl << "Error state = " << file.rdstate( ) ;
        cout << endl << "good( ) = " << file.good( ) ;
        cout << endl << "eof( ) = " << file.eof( ) ;
        cout << endl << "fail( ) = " << file.fail( ) ;
        cout << endl << "bad( ) = " << file.bad( ) ;
}
```

While opening the file using *open( )* function, it may result into success or failure so it is checked using the statement *if (! file)*. If we are unable to open the file then *file* gets replaced with 0 (Refer Q 9.22). If the condition *if (! file)* is satisfied then we have called a function *check( )* to check as to which particular error has occurred. In the function *check( )* we can easily ascertain the type of error by calling the function which returns the status of state variable bits. For details of state variable bits refer Q 9.25.

Q 9.37

How can we copy the contents of one file to another in one shot?

Ans

This is shown in the following program:

```
#include <fstream.h>

void main( )
{
    char source [ 67 ], target [ 67 ] ;
    char ch ;

    cout << endl << "Enter source filename" ;
    cin >> source ;

    cout << endl << "Enter target filename" ;
    cin >> target ;

    ifstream  infile ( source ) ;
```

```
    ofstream  outfile ( target ) ;

    outfile << infile.rdbuf( ) ;
}
```

Here all the copying is done through the single statement

```
outfile << infile.rdbuf( ) ;
```

The function *rdbuf( )* returns a pointer to the buffer stream. Refer
Q 9.41 (m) for more detailed information.

Q 9.38

What is *strstream*?

Ans

strstream is a type of input/output stream that works with the
memory. It allows using section of the memory as a stream object.
These streams provide the classes that can be used for storing the
stream of bytes into memory. For example, we can store integers,
floats and strings as a stream of bytes.

There are several classes that implement this in-memory
formatting. The class *ostrstream* derived from *ostream* is used
when output is to be sent to memory, the class *istrstream* derived
from *istream* is used when input is taken from memory and
strstream class derived from *iostream* is used for memory objects
that do both input and output.

Q 9.39

Where is the *istrstream* class used?

Ans

When we want to retrieve the streams of bytes from memory we can use *istrstream*. The following example shows the use of *istrstream* class.

```cpp
#include <strstream.h>

void main( )
{
    int  age ;
    float salary ;
    char  name [ 50 ] ;
    char  str[ ] = "22 12004.50 Ravi Sudhir Joshi" ;

    istrstream  s ( str ) ;

    s >> age >> salary >> name ;

    cout << age << endl
         << salary << endl
         << name ;

    cout << endl << s.rdbuf( ) ;
}
```

Here, *s* is the object of the class *istrstream*. When we are creating the object *s*, the constructor of *istrstream* gets called that receives a pointer to the zero terminated character array *str*. The statement *s >> age >> salary >> name* extracts the *age*, *salary* and the *name* from the *istrstream* object *s*. However, while extracting the name, only the first name gets extracted. The balance is extracted using *rdbuf( )*.

Q 9.40

When is the *ostrstream::freeze( )* function used?

Ans

While outputting data to memory in the in-memory formatting we need to create an object of the class *ostrstream*. The constructor of *ostrstream* receives the address of the buffer but if we want that the *ostrstream* object should do its own memory management then we need to create an *ostrstream* object with no constructor arguments as:

ostrstream s ;

Now *s* will do its own memory management. We can stuff as many bytes into it as we want. If it falls short of memory, it will allocate more memory. If it cannot, it may even move the block of memory. When the object goes out of scope, the heap storage is automatically released. This is a more flexible approach if we do not know how much space we are going to need.

If we want the physical address of the memory used by *s*, we can obtain it by calling the *str( )* member function:

char* p = s.str( ) ;

Once *str( )* has been called then the block of memory allocated by *ostrstream* cannot be moved. This is logical. It can't move the block since we are now expecting it to be at a particular location. In such a case we say that *ostrstream* has frozen itself. Once frozen we can't add any more characters to it. Adding characters to a frozen *ostrstream* results in undefined behavior. In addition, the *ostrstream* is no longer responsible for cleaning up the storage. You took over that responsibility when you asked for the *char ** with *str( )*.

We can clean the storage in two ways:

– Using the *delete* operator as shown below:

```
ostrstream s ;
char *p ;
```

```
p = s.str( ) ;
delete p ;
```

− By unfreezing the *ostrstream*. You do this by calling *freeze( )*, with an argument 1. During freezing it is called with the default argument of 0.

Q 9.41

State whether the following statements are True or False:

(a) In the *iostream* library the *ios* class is at the root of the class hierarchy.

Ans

True. The *ios* (I/O specification) class contains features that are common to all input/output stream classes. It includes the flags for formatting the input/output data, the error-status flags and the file operation modes.

(b) Some of the *ios* flags can be set either through the *setf( )* function or through the manipulators.

Ans

False. The *setf( )* function is used to set the *ios* flags but manipulators directly insert the formatting instructions into the stream.

(c) *ios* class does buffer management.

Ans

False. The *streambuf* class does buffer management.

(d) Only for those manipulators which need an argument, we need to include the file 'iomanip.h'.

Ans

True. Manipulators without arguments are provided in "iostream.h", whereas, those that take arguments are provided in "iomanip.h".

(e) We can unset manipulators using *unsetf( )* function.

Ans

False. Manipulators can never be unset.

(f) When we are using a manipulator we are in fact calling a function.

Ans

True.

(g) It is possible to create your own manipulators.

Ans

True. For creating your own manipulator refer to question numbers Q 9.43 to Q 9.45.

(h) The *istream_withassign* class has been derived from the *istream* class and overloaded assignment operator has been added to it.

Ans

True. The *_withassign* classes are much like their base classes except that they include overloaded assignment operators. Using these operators the objects of the *_withassign* classes can be copied. The *istream, ostream,* and *iostream* classes are made uncopyable by making their overloaded copy constructor and assignment operators *private*.

(i)   *cout* is an object of *ostream* class.

Ans

False. *cout* is an object of *ostream_withassign* class.

(j)   *cout*, *cin* and *cprn* are predefined stream objects.

Ans

False. There is no such thing as *cprn*. There are four predefined stream objects: *cin*, *cout*, *cerr* and *clog*. *cin* and *cout* are objects of *istream_withassign* and *ostream_withassign* classes respectively. These objects are used for keyboard input and screen display respectively. *cerr* is an object of *ostream_withassign* class and is used for displaying error messages. *clog* is an object of the class *ostream_withassign* and is used for logging messages. It is a fully buffered version of *cerr*.

(k)   We can use *cerr* in the place of *cout*.

Ans

True. Usually the *cerr* object is used to display error messages on the screen and to diagnose our program. Output of *cerr* cannot be redirected. Output sent to *cout* is buffered, whereas the one sent to *cerr* is displayed immediately.

(l)   Objects can read and write themselves.

Ans

True. This can be explained with the help of following example:

```
#include <fstream.h>
#include <iostream.h>
```

```
class employee
{
    private :

        char name [ 20 ] ;
        int age ;
        float salary ;

    public :

        void getdata( )
        {
            cout << "Enter name, age and salary of employee : " ;
            cin >> name >> age >> salary ;
        }

        void store( )
        {
            ofstream file ;
            file.open ( "EMPLOYEE.DAT", ios::app | ios::binary ) ;
            file.write ( ( char * ) this, sizeof ( *this ) ) ;
            file.close( ) ;
        }

        void retrieve ( int n )
        {
            ifstream file ;
            file.open ( "EMPLOYEE.DAT", ios::binary ) ;
            file.seekg ( n * sizeof ( employee ) ) ;
            file.read ( ( char * ) this, sizeof ( *this ) ) ;
            file.close( ) ;
        }

        void show( )
        {
            cout << "Name : " << name
                << endl << "Age : " << age
                << endl << "Salary :" << salary << endl ;
```

```
        }
};

void main( )
{
    employee e [ 5 ];

    for ( int  i = 0 ; i <= 4 ; i++ )
    {
        e [ i ].getdata( );
        e [ i ].store( );
    }

    for ( i = 0 ; i <= 4 ; i++ )
    {
        e [ i ].retrieve ( i );
        e [ i ].show( );
    }
}
```

Here, *employee* is the class whose objects can write and read themselves. The *getdata( )* function has been used to get the data of employee and store it in the data members *name, age* and *salary.* The *store( )* function is used to write an object to the file. In this function a file has been opened in append mode and each time data of current object has been stored after the last record (if any) in the file.

Function *retrieve( )* is used to get the data of a particular employee from the file. This retrieved data has been stored in the data members *name, age* and *salary.* Here *this* has been used to store data since it contains the address of the current object. The function *show( )* has been used to display the data of employee.

(m) *strstream*s serve the same purpose as *sprintf( )* and *sscanf( ).*

Ans

True. This can be explained with the help of following example:

```cpp
#include <iostream.h>
#include <strstream.h>
#include <iomanip.h>

void main( )
{
    char  ch = 'Z' ;
    int  i = 25 ;
    float  a = 5.375f ;
    char  str[ ] = "strstreams at work" ;

    char  buff [ 100 ] ;

    ostrstream  s ( buff, 100 ) ;

    s << endl
      << "ch = " << ch << endl
      << "i = " << i << endl
      << "a = " << a << endl
      << "str = " << str
      << ends ;

    cout << s.rdbuf( ) ;
}
```

The output of the program would be:

```
ch = Z
i = 25
a = 5.375
str = strstreams at work
```

s is object of the type *ostrstream*. When *s* is created using two-argument constructor the base address and length of the string *buff* is passed to its constructor. This *buff* string is acting as a buffer for storing values. The value of variables *ch*, *i*, *a* and *str* are stored in the buffer using the object *s*. The *ends* manipulator is used to terminate the string *buff* with a character '\0'. Finally all the values are printed through the statement

```
cout << s.rdbuf( ) ;
```

When we call *rdbuf( )* it returns the address of the *strstreambuf* where the values are stored. The *get* pointer inside the *streambuf* is moved forward as the characters are displayed. The other way to display the characters is to directly print the content of the string *buff* through *cout*.

(n) The *istream::getline( )* function cannot tackle multi-words strings.

Ans

False. The *getline( )* function can read one line at a time. This function is a member of *istream* (from which *ifstream* is derived). It reads characters until it encounters the end of line character, '\n', and places the resulting string in the buffer supplied as an argument. The prototype of this function is as follows:

```
istream& getline ( signed char*, int, char = '\n' ) ;
```

The second parameter is the maximum size of the buffer. The third parameter is optional which is the string terminator with default value '\n'. Any other value can also be passed to act as a string terminator.

(o) *seekg( )* is a *istream* class member function.

Ans

True. *seekg( )* moves the *get* file pointer to the specified position.

(p) The default opening mode of *fstream* is *ios::in | ios::out*.

Ans

False. There is no default opening mode. We need to explicitly define the opening mode of the *fstream* either through the constructor or through the *open( )* function.

(q) While writing binary data to a file we must specify delimiters to differentiate the data.

Ans

False. Binary data is always stored in terms of bytes. The functions used to read or write the binary data don't care how the data is formatted. They simply transfer a buffer full of bytes from and to a disk file.

(r) If the character '\x0C' is sent to *stdprn* it causes the page to eject from the printer?

Ans

True. Refer Q 9.51 for a program that shows how to send the form-feed ('\x0C') character to the printer.

Q 9.42

What will be the output of the following programs:

(a)
```
#include <iostream.h>
void main( )
{
```

```
    char  str[ ] = "The boring stuff" ;
    char  *p = "That's interesting" ;
    cout << endl << str ;
    cout << endl << p ;

    cout << endl << ( void * ) str ;
    cout << endl << ( void * ) p ;
}
```

Ans

The output would be:

```
The boring stuff
That's interesting
0x8fa20fea
0x8f550011
```

In the first *cout* statement the base address of *str* gets passed which prints the string "The boring stuff". In the second *cout* statement pointer *p* is passed which is a pointer to the constant string "That's interesting". Hence the string "That's interesting" gets printed.

In the third and fourth *cout* statements the address of *str* and the one stored in *p* are typecast into *void* * and hence instead of strings their respective addresses gets printed.

(b)
```
#include <iostream.h>
#include <iomanip.h>
void main( )
{
    int i = 10 ;
    float  a = 425.123f ;
    cout << setiosflags ( ios::showbase | ios::uppercase ) ;
    cout << hex << i << endl ;
    cout.precision ( 4 ) ;
```

```
    cout << setiosflags ( ios::showpoint ) << a ,
}
```

Ans

The output would be:

```
0XA
425.1230
```

The *setiosflags( )* is a manipulator which sets the format flags according to the argument passed to it.

The *showbase* is the base indicator for numbers. For example, 0 for octal, 0x for hex. The *uppercase* displays the uppercase A-F for hex values and E for scientific values. Hence in the output 0XA, 0X is base indicator and A is hex equivalent of decimal 10 which appears in uppercase.

The function *precision( )* sets floating-point precision. The default precision is six digits.

The precision indicates the number of digits after the decimal point only if the display format is scientific or fixed. If the format is neither floating-point nor fixed then the precision indicates the total number of significant digits.

The flag *showpoint* shows decimal point and trailing zeros for float in the output.

(c)
```cpp
#include <iostream.h>
void main( )
{
    char  str[ ] = "Just listing" ;
    cout.width ( 40 ) ;
    cout << str << endl ;
    cout.setf ( ios::left, ios::adjustfield ) ;
    cout.width ( 40 ) ;
    cout << str ;
```

```
}
```

Ans

The output would be:

                              Just listing
Just listing

By default a string is always right justified. The *width( )* sets the field-width. The string "Just listing" gets printed with right justification within the 40 spaces set by *width( )*. The *setf( )* sets the formatting flags. Here, it sets the string justification to left. The flags *left, right* and *internal* are collectively referred to as *adjustfield*.

Q 9.43

Write your own zero-argument manipulator that should work same as hex.

Ans

The program is as follows:

```
#include <iostream.h>

ostream& myhex ( ostream &o )
{
    o.setf ( ios::hex ) ;
    return o ;
}

void main( )
{
    cout << endl << myhex << 2000 ;
}
```

Q 9.44

Create the following one-argument manipulators:

- dollar
- pound
- euro

These manipulators should take amount in dollar/pound/euro and return the value in rupees.

Ans

Note that we have assumed suitable values to convert amount in dollar/pound/euro into rupees.

```
#include <iostream.h>

class dollar
{
    private :

        float re ;

    public :

        dollar ( float n )
        {
            re = n ;
        }

        friend ostream& operator << ( ostream& o, dollar& s )
        {
            o << 48.36f * s.re ;
            return o ;
        }
} ;

class pound
```

```
{
    private :

        float re ;

    public :

        pound ( float n )
        {
            re = n ;
        }

        friend ostream& operator << ( ostream& o, pound& s )
        {
            o << 68.54 * s.re ;
            return o ;
        }
} ;

class euro
{
    private :

        float re ;

    public :

        euro ( float n )
        {
            re = n ;
        }

        friend ostream& operator << ( ostream& o, euro& s )
        {
            o << 41.98f * s.re ;
            return o ;
        }
} ;
```

```
void main( )
{
    cout << dollar ( 1 ) << endl ;
    cout << pound ( 1 ) << endl ;
    cout << euro ( 1 ) << endl ;
}
```

For a detailed explanation of *friend* functions please refer Q 10.5.

Q 9.45

Write a program that will create a manipulator with arguments. If row number and column number are passed as arguments to this manipulator, it should position the cursor at that row and column.

Ans

The program is as follows:

```
#include <iostream.h>
#include <conio.h>

class setcur
{
    private :

        int  row, col ;

    public :

        setcur ( int  r, int  c )
        {
            row = r ;
            col = c ;
        }

        friend ostream& operator << ( ostream&  o, setcur&  sc )
        {
            gotoxy ( sc.row, sc.col ) ;
```

```
                return o ;
            }
};

void main( )
{
    clrscr( ) ;
    cout << setcur ( 12, 12 ) << "I am here." ;
}
```

Q 9.46

Write a program to write the standard data types to a disk file then read them back and finally display them on the screen.

Ans

The program is as follows:

```
#include <fstream.h>

void main( )
{
    ofstream  outfile ( "SAMPLE.TXT" ) ;

    char  ch = 'V' ;
    int  i = 24 ;
    float  a = 5000.079f ;
    char  str[ ] = "Spirit" ;

    outfile << ch << endl << i << endl << a << endl << str ;
    outfile.close( ) ;

    ifstream  infile ( "SAMPLE.TXT" ) ;
    infile >> ch >> i >> a >> str ;

    cout << ch << endl << i << endl << a << endl << str ;
}
```

Q 9.47

Write a program that takes the name of a text file from user and prints its size in bytes.

Ans

The program is as follows:

```
#include <fstream.h>
#include <iostream.h>

void main( )
{
    char str [ 67 ] ;

    cout << "Enter the file name :" ;
    cin >> str ;

    ifstream  file ( str ) ;

    if ( ! file )
    {
        cout << "Cannot open file" ;
        return ;
    }

    file.seekg ( 0, ios::end ) ;
    long  size = file.tellg( ) ;

    cout << "Size of file in bytes = " << size ;
}
```

Q 9.48

Write a program to compare two files containing same type of records. For this, declare a class having data members similar to the record fields. Overload == operator in the class to compare the records.

Ans

The program is as follows:

```
#include <fstream.h>
#include <string.h>

class book
{
    char  name [ 30 ] ;
    float  price ;
    int  pages ;

    public :

        int operator == ( book  &b )
        {
            return ( ( ! strcmp ( name, b.name ) ) && ( price == b.price )
                    && ( pages == b.pages ) ) ;
        }
} ;

void  main( )
{
    book  b1, b2 ;

    ifstream  i1 ( "bnames1.dat" ) ;
    ifstream  i2 ( "bnames2.dat" ) ;

    int  flag = 1 ;
    while ( 1 )
    {
        i1.read ( ( ( char* ) &b1, sizeof ( book ) ) ;
        i2.read ( ( ( char* ) &b2, sizeof ( book ) ) ;

        if ( i1.eof( ) || i2.eof( ) )
            break ;
```

```
            if ( b1 == b2 )
                continue ;
            else
            {
                cout << "Files are not same" ;
                flag = 0 ;
                break ;
            }
        }

    if ( flag )
        cout << "Files are same" ;
}
```

Q 9.49

Develop a program to search for a word in a file and replace it with the specified word. The user should be able to specify the old word and the new word.

Ans

The program is as follows:

```
#include <fstream.h>
#include <string.h>
#include <stdio.h>

void main( )
{
    char ch, fname [ 13 ], oword [ 10 ], nword [ 10 ] ;
    cout << "Enter the file name" ;
    cin >> fname ;
    cout << "Enter old word" ;
    cin >> oword ;
    cout << "Enter new word" ;
    cin >> nword ;

    ifstream  i ( fname ) ;
```

```
ofstream  o ( "temp.txt" ) ;

int  match, len ;

while ( 1 )
{
    i.get ( ch ) ;
    if ( i.eof( ) )
        break ;
    if ( ch != oword [ 0 ] )
    {
        o.put ( ch ) ;
        continue ;
    }
    else
    {
        match = 1 ;
        len = 1 ;
        for ( int  j = 1 ; j < strlen ( oword ) ; j++ )
        {
            len++ ;
            i.get ( ch ) ;
            if ( ch != oword [ j ] )
            {
                match = 0 ;
                break ;
            }
        }
    }

    if ( match == 1 )
    {
        for ( int  k = 0 ; k < strlen ( nword ) ; k++ )
            o.put ( nword [ k ] ) ;
    }
    else
    {
        i.seekg ( - ( len ), ios::cur ) ;
```

```
        for ( int I = 0 ; I < len ; I++ )
        {
            i.get ( ch ) ;
            o.put ( ch ) ;
        }
    }
}

i.close( ) ;
o.close( ) ;

remove ( fname ) ;
rename ( "temp.txt", fname ) ;
}
```

Q 9.50

There are 100 records present in a file with each record containing a 6-character item code, a 20-character item name and an integer quantity. Write a program to read these records, arrange them in ascending order and write them in the same file overwriting the earlier records.

Ans

The program is as follows:

```
#include <fstream.h>
#include <stdlib.h>
#include <stdio.h>

// comparison function for qsort( )
int fun ( const void *x, const void *y )
{
    char *x1 = ( char * ) x ;
    char *y1 = ( char * ) y ;
    return *x1 - *y1 ;
}
```

```
class record
{
    private :

        struct item
        {
            char  code [ 7 ] ;
            char  name [ 21 ] ;
            int  quantity ;
        } *p ;

        const int  noofrec ;
        fstream  file ;

    public :

        record ( int  n ) : noofrec ( n )
        {
            p = new item [ n ] ;
        }

        void getrec( )
        {
            file.open ( "EMP.DAT", ios::binary | ios::in | ios::out ) ;

            if ( ! file )
            {
                cout << endl << "Unable to open file" ;
                exit ( 0 ) ;
            }

            item  *temp = p ;
            while ( file.read ( ( char * ) temp, sizeof ( item ) ) )
                temp++ ;

            file.close( ) ;
        }
```

```
void sortrec( )
{
    qsort ( p, noofrec, sizeof ( item ), fun ) ;
}

void setrec( )
{
    file.open ( "TEMP.DAT", ios::binary | ios::in | ios::out ) ;

    if ( ! file )
    {
        cout << endl << "Unable to open file" ;
        exit ( 0 ) ;
    }

    item *temp = p ;
    for ( int  i = 0 ; i < noofrec ; i++ )
    {
        file.write ( ( char * ) temp, sizeof ( item ) ) ;
        temp++ ;
    }

    file.close( ) ;
}

~record( )
{
    delete [ ] p ;
    remove ( "EMP.DAT" ) ;
    rename ( "TEMP.DAT", "EMP.DAT" ) ;
}

} ;

void main( )
{
    record  r ( 100 ) ;
```

```
        r.getrec( ) ;
        r.sortrec( ) ;
        r.setrec( ) ;
}
```

Q 9.51

Write a program to print the contents of a disk file on the printer?

Ans

The program is as follows:

```
#include <fstream.h>
#include <iostream.h>
#include <stdlib.h>

int main( )
{
    char filename [ 67 ] ;

    cout << endl << "Enter filename" ;
    cin >> filename ;

    ifstream infile ( filename ) ;
    if ( ! infile )
    {
        cerr << endl << "Unable to open file" ;
        exit ( 1 ) ;
    }

    ofstream outfile ( "PRN" ) ;
    if ( ! outfile )
    {
        cerr << endl << "Unable to open file" ;
        exit ( 2 ) ·
    }

    char ch ;
```

```
while ( infile.get ( ch ) != 0 )
    outfile.put ( ch ) ;

outfile.put ( '\x0C' ) ;
}
```

For sending the output to printer we have opened a file by the name PRN, where "PRN" is name given to the first parallel printer.

Advanced Features

Q 10.1

What is *kind of* and *has a* relationship?

Ans

There are two types of relationships that relate two classes. One is *kind of* and another is *has a* relationship. When a class is derived from another class, it is said to be *kind of* its base class. This is nothing but inheritance.

The *has a* relationship is supported by composition or containership. In *has a* relationship we simply create object of a class as a data member of any other class.

Q 10.2

What is iterator and iteration?

Ans

An iterator is an object that moves through the container accessing each element in the container. The process of moving from element to element in the container is called iteration.

Q 10.3

When should the *explicit* keyword be used in the constructor? Can it be used with any other function?

Ans

When we want that the constructor should build the objects but it should not get used for carrying out conversions. At such times we are required to use the *explicit* keyword with the constructor. This is shown in the following example:

```
#include <iostream.h>

class sample
{
    private :

        int i ;

    public :

        explicit sample ( int  ii = 0 )
        {
            i = ii ;
        }

        sample operator + ( sample  s )
        {
            sample t ;
            t.i = i + s.i ;
            return t ;
        }

        void display( )
        {
            cout << i ;
        }
```

```
};

void main( )
{
    sample  s1 ( 15 ), s2 ;
    s2 = s1 + 25 ;
    s2.display( ) ;
}
```

This code would not compile. At the time of compilation of the statement,

```
s2 = s1 + 25 ;
```

the compiler would search for the overloaded *operator + ( )* functions. When it finds that there is a wrong type on the right hand side of + it would look for a conversion function that can convert an *int* to *sample*. The one-argument constructor can meet this requirement. Hence the compiler would decide to call it. This is an implicit conversion, one that you may not have intended to make possible. We can prevent such implicit conversions by declaring the constructor as *explicit*. With this keyword in place, now the compiler would report that it could not do the conversion.

There is one small disadvantage, however. We can no longer create objects by saying,

```
sample s3 = 25 ;
```

Also, the keyword *explicit* can be used only with constructors.

Q 10.4
How would you change a data member of the *const* object?

Ans

To change the data members of the *const* object, the data members are declared as *mutable* in the class. This is shown in the following example:

```cpp
#include <iostream.h>

class sample
{
    private :

        mutable int i ;

    public :

        sample ( int ii = 0 )
        {
            i = ii ;
        }

        void fun( ) const
        {
            i++ ;
            cout << i ;
        }
};

void main( )
{
    const sample  s ( 15 ) ;
    s.fun( ) ;
}
```

Here, the object *s* is *const* and hence only *const* functions can operate upon it. When the *const* function *fun( )* gets called to operate upon object *s*, the data member *i* is incremented. Ideally the data member should not be changed, as object is defined as *const*. But we can change the data member *i* because it is declared as *mutable* in the class *sample*.

Q 10.5

What is a *friend* function and when should a function be made *friend*?

Ans

A global function that can access all the data members of a class is called a *friend* function of that class. To make any function a *friend* of some class it must be declared with a keyword *friend* in that class. A *friend* function acts as a bridge between two classes.

A function is made *friend* in the following two cases:

– To access private data of a class from a non-member function.
– To increase the versatility of overloaded operators.

Q 10.6

How does a *friend* function help in increasing the versatility of overloaded operators?

Ans

Consider the following statement,

s2 = s1 * 2 ;

where, *s1* and *s2* are objects of *sample* class. This statement works if the overloaded *operator * (sample s)* or conversion function is provided in the class. Internally this statement becomes,

s2 = s1.operator * (2) ;

The function materializes because it is called with an object *s1*. The *this* pointer of *s1* implicitly gets passed. To collect 2 in *s*, compiler firstly calls the one-argument constructor, builds the nameless object, then it gets collected in *s*. Hence it works properly.

But if we write the above statement as,

s2 = 2 * s1 ;

then it won't compile. This is because the call now is treated as,

s2 = 2.operator * (s1) ;

and 2 is not an object.

The *friend* function helps to get rid of such a situation as shown in the following example:

```
#include <iostream.h>

class sample
{
    private :

        int i ;

    public :

        sample ( int ii = 0 )
        {
            i = ii ;
        }

        void showdata( )
        {
            cout << i << endl ;
        }

        friend sample operator * ( sample, sample ) ;
};

sample operator * ( sample s1, sample s2 )
```

```
{
    sample temp ;

    temp.i = s1.i * s2.i ;
    return ( temp ) ;
}

void main( )
{
    sample  s1 ( 10 ), s2 ;

    s2 = s1 * 2 ;
    s2.showdata( ) ;

    s1 = 2 * s2 ;
    s1.showdata( ) ;
}
```

Earlier the *operator *( )* function took only one argument, whereas here it takes two. This is because the operator function is no longer a member function of the class. It is a *friend* of the class *example*. Thus the statement

s2 = s1 * 2 ;

doesn't take the form *s1.operator * (2)*.

This example shows that using *friend* permits the overloaded operators to be more versatile.

Q 10.7

What is forward referencing and when should it be used?

Ans

Consider the following program:

class test

```
{
    public :

        friend void fun ( sample, test ) ;
} ;

class sample
{
    public :

        friend void fun ( sample, test ) ;

} ;

void fun ( sample  s, test  t )
{
    // code
}

void main( )
{
    sample  s ;
    test  t ;
    fun ( s, t ) ;
}
```

This program would not compile. It gives an error that *sample* is undeclared identifier in the statement,

```
friend void fun ( sample, test ) ;
```

of the class *test*. This is so because the class *sample* is defined below the class *test* and we are using it before its definition. To overcome this error we need to give forward reference of the class *sample* before the definition of class *test*. The following statement is the forward reference of class *sample*.

```
class sample ;
```

Forward referencing is generally required when we make a class or a function as a *friend*.

Q 10.8

Write one case where *friend* function becomes necessary.

Ans

When we want that an object of a user-defined type should be printed using *cout* then it is necessary to overload *operator* << ( ). This function is declared as *friend* in the class whose object we want to print. Refer Q 10.30 for more details.

Q 10.9

Can we make a class as a *friend*?

Ans

Yes. If we make the entire class as a *friend* then automatically all the member functions and data members of the class become *friend*s. Hence we can access all of them. Q 10.26 (e) shows an example program where a class is declared as a *friend* of another class.

Q 10.10

Is it necessary that while using pointer to member with data, the data must be made *public*?

Ans

Yes. The *private* data members are never accessible outside the class.

Q 10.11

How would you define a pointer to data member of the type pointer to pointer?

Ans

This is shown in the following program:

```cpp
#include <iostream.h>

class sample
{
    public :

        sample ( int **pp )
        {
            p = pp ;
        }

        int **p ;
};

int **sample::*ptr = &sample::p ;

void main( )
{
    int i = 9 ;
    int *pi = &i ;

    sample s ( &pi ) ;
    cout << ** ( s.*ptr ) ;
}
```

Here, *ptr* is the pointer to data member *p,* which is of the type pointer to integer pointer.

Q 10.12

Can we create a pointer to member function?

Ans

Yes. This is shown in the following example:

```
#include <iostream.h>

class sample
{
    public :

        void fun( )
        {
            cout << "fun with pointers" ;
        }
};

void ( sample::*pfun ) ( ) = &sample::fun ;

void main( )
{
    sample  s ;
    ( s.*pfun ) ( ) ;
}
```

Here, *pfun* is pointer to member function *fun( )* of the class *sample*.

Q 10.13

What is an array of pointers to member functions and what is its limitation?

Ans

The following program shows how to create an array of pointers to member functions:

```
#include <iostream.h>

class sample
```

```
{
    public :

        void fun1( )
        {
            cout << "fun1" << endl ;
        }

        void fun2( )
        {
            cout << "fun2" << endl ;
        }

        void fun3( )
        {
            cout << "fun3" << endl ;
        }
};

void ( sample::*pfun [ 3] ) ( ) = {
                                    &sample::fun1,
                                    &sample::fun2,
                                    &sample::fun3
                        } ;

void main( )
{
    sample  s ;
    for ( int  i = 0 ; i <= 2 ; i++ )
        ( s.*pfun [ i ] ) ( ) ;
}
```

Here, *pfun* is an array of pointers to member functions which holds the address of the functions *fun1( )*, *fun2( )* and *fun3( )*.

The limitation of the array of pointers to member functions is that we cannot store the addresses of the different type of functions in it. All the functions whose addresses it contains should have the same prototype.

Q 10.14

What is a *namespace*?

Ans

While developing a program different header files are included. It may happen that some header files may contain same function or class names. Trying to access these functions or classes may lead to an ambiguity. Such ambiguity can be avoided using *namespaces*.

C++ provides a single global namespace. We can subdivide the global namespace into more manageable pieces using the *namespace* feature of C++. Because of *namespace* feature it becomes possible to use the same name in separate namespaces without conflict. As long as they appear in separate namespaces, each name will be unique because of the addition of the *namespace* identifier.

Following are few useful points you must know about *namespaces*:

- The declarations that fall outside all *namespaces* are still members of the global *namespace*.
- A *namespace* definition can be nested within another *namespace* definition. For example:

```
namespace outer
{
    int a = 17 ;
    int fun2( ) ;

    namespace inner
    {
```

```
        int  b = 9 ;
    }
}
```

- Definition of functions or member functions that are declared in a *namespace* can be done outside the *namespace*. This is shown in the following example:

```cpp
#include <iostream.h>

namespace name
{
    class sample
    {
        public :
            void fun( ) ;
    };
}

void name::sample::fun( )
{
    cout << "fun with namespace" ;
}

void main( )
{
    name::sample  s ;
    s.fun( ) ;
}
```

Q 10.15

If two header files contain the same function names or class names then how would you avoid the clash of names if both the files are to be included?

Ans

We can avoid the clash of function or class names by defining them in different *namespaces*. This is shown in the following code snippet:

```
// file1.h
namespace name1
{
    class sample
    {
        // code
    };
}
// file2.h
namespace name2
{
    class sample
    {
        // code
    };
}
```

To differentiate between the classes *sample* that are present in "file1.h" and "file2.h" we need to use them through the syntax *name1::sample* and *name2::sample*.

Q 10.16

How would you give an alternate name to a *namespace*?

Ans

An alternate name given to a *namespace* is called a namespace-alias. Namespace-alias is generally used to save the typing effort when the names of *namespace*s are very long or complex. The following syntax is used to give an alias to a *namespace*.

```
namespace  myname = my_old_very_long_name ;
```

Q 10.17

How to refer to a name of class or function that is defined within a namespace?

Ans

There are two ways in which we can refer to a name of class or function that is defined within a namespace:

- Using scope resolution operator
- Through the *using* keyword

This is shown in the following example:

```
namespace name1
{
    class sample1
    {
        // code
    };
}

namespace name2
{
    class sample2
    {
        // code
    };
}

using namespace name2 ;

void main( )
```

```
{
    name1::sample1 s1 ;
    sample2 s2 ;
}
```

In this example class *sample1* is referred using the scope resolution operator. On the other hand we can directly refer to class *sample2* because of the statement

using namespace name2 ;

The *using* keyword declares all the names in the namespace to be in the current scope. So we can use the names without any qualifiers.

Q 10.18

What is RTTI?

Ans

RTTI stands for *Run Time Type Identification*. In an inheritance hierarchy, using RTTI we can find the exact type of the object using a pointer or reference to the base class. The idea behind virtual functions is to upcast the derived class object's address into a pointer to a base class object and then let the virtual function mechanism implement the correct behaviour for that type. Does this mean that an attempt to know the type of the derived class object from the base class pointer (RTTI) a step backward? No. At times it is useful to know the exact type of the object from the base class pointer. You may require this information to perform some specific operation more efficiently.

Q 10.19

How to get the information about the object at runtime?

Ans

There are two ways to get the information about the object at runtime they are as follows:

– Using *typeid( )* operator
– Using the *dynamic_cast* operator

The following example shows how to use the operator *typeid( )*.

```
#include <typeinfo.h>
#include <iostream.h>

class sample
{
    // code
};

void main( )
{
    sample s ;
    cout << typeid ( s ).name( ) ;
}
```

The operator *typeid( )* takes an object *s* and returns a reference to a global *const* object of the type *type_info*, then function *name( )* is called to get the name of the class of the object. To use the *type_info* object's reference we need to include the header file "typeinfo.h".

The *dynamic_cast* operator can also be used to get the information of the object at runtime. This is shown in the following example.

```
#include <typeinfo.h>
#include <iostream.h>

class base
{
    public :
```

```
            virtual void fun1( )
            {
            }
} ;

class derived1 : public base
{
} ;

class derived2 : public base
{
} ;

void main( )
{
    base  *b ;
    derived1  d1, *p ;
    b = &d1 ;

    if ( p = dynamic_cast <derived1 *> ( b ) )
        cout << endl << "Of type derived1" ;
    else
        cout << endl << "Not of type derived1" ;

    derived2 d2 ;
    b = &d2 ;

    if ( p = dynamic_cast <derived1 *> ( b ) )
        cout << endl << "Of type derived1" ;
    else
        cout << endl << "Not of type derived1" ;
}
```

The output of the program would be:

```
Of type derived1
Not of type derived1
```

The *dynamic_cast* operator attempts to convert the pointer *b* which initially contains the address object *d1*. If the result is non-zero then *b* was indeed pointing to object of the type *derived1*. If the result is zero it means it pointed to something else. Hence the output.

Q 10.20

Would the following program work?

```
#include <typeinfo.h>
#include <iostream.h>

void main( )
{
    cout << typeid ( 9 ).name( ) ;
}
```

Ans

Yes. The output of the program is *int*. It prints the type of constant passed to it, which is nothing but an integer constant.

Q 10.21

Can we get the *typeid* of *void* pointers?

Ans

No. At runtime, type identification doesn't work with *void* pointers, because *void* * truly means no type information at all.

Q 10.22

Why do we get strange and misleading errors while running the program involving *typeid* on VC++ 6.0 compiler?

Ans

The errors occur because we may not have enabled the RTTI option. To overcome these errors we need to perform the following steps.

- Select 'Settings' from the 'Project' menu and click the 'C/C++' tab.
- From the category listbox, select 'C++ language'.
- Click the checkbox named 'Enable Run-time Type Information'.

Q 10.23

What is a *const_cast*?

Ans

The *const_cast* is used to convert a *const* to a non-*const*. This is shown in the following program:

```
#include <iostream.h>

void main( )
{
    const int a = 0 ;

    int *ptr = ( int * ) &a ;  // one way
    ptr = const_cast <int *> ( &a ) ;  // better way
}
```

Here, the address of the *const* variable *a* is assigned to the pointer to a non-*const* variable.

The *const_cast* is also used when we want to change the data members of a class inside the *const* member functions. The following code snippet shows this:

```
class sample
{
    private :

        int  data ;
    public :

        void fun( ) const
        {
            ( const_cast <sample *> ( this ) ) -> data = 70 ;
        }
};
```

Q 10.24

What is a *reinterpret_cast*?

Ans

If for some reason we need to assign one kind of pointer type to
another, then we can use *reinterpret_cast*. The *reinterpret_cast*
can also be used to convert pointers to integers or vice versa (Refer
Q 10.29).

Q 10.25

What is a *static_cast*?

Ans

The *static_cast* is used when we want well-defined conversions
like:

– castless conversions
– narrowing conversions
– conversion from void *
– implicit type conversions

The following example shows how to make all these conversions.

```
#include <iostream.h>

class base
{
};

class derived : public base
{
    public :

        operator int( )
        {
            return 1 ;
        }
};

class sample
{
};

void main( )
{
    int  i = 10 ;
    long  l ;
    float  f ;

    // castless conversion - safe
    l = i ;
    f = i ;

    cout << endl << l << f ;

    // explicit conversion - safe
    l = static_cast <long> ( i ) ;
    f = static_cast <float> ( i ) ;
```

```
        cout << endl << l << f ;

        // narrowing conversions
        i = l ;
        cout << endl << i ;
        i = f ;
        cout << endl << i ;

        // better way of doing narrowing conversions
        i = static_cast <int> ( l ) ;
        i = static_cast <int> ( f ) ;

        void *vptr ;
        float *fptr ;

        // dangerous conversion through a void pointer
        vptr = &i ;
        fptr = ( float * ) vptr ;
        fptr = static_cast <float *> ( vptr ) ;

        derived d ;
        base *bptr ;

        // upcasting - safe
        bptr = &d ;
        // explicit upcasting - safe
        bptr = static_cast <base *> ( &d ) ;

        int x ;

        // conversion through a conversion function
        x = d ;
        // more explicit conversion through a conversion function
        x = static_cast <int> ( d ) ;

        sample *sptr = ( sample * ) bptr ;
        // sample *ptr = static_cast <sample *> ( bptr ) ; // error
}
```

In the last two statements when we try to cast a pointer to *base* into a pointer to *sample* using *static_cast* an error is flashed. This is so because *static_cast* won't allow the cast out of the hierarchy. However, the traditional cast would permit this. It means *static_cast* is safer than traditional casting.

Q 10.26

State whether the following statements are True or False:

(a) The *phenomenon* of writing a class within a class is known as composition.

Ans

False. Composition is creating an object of an existing class within another class. For example:

```
class money
{
};

class bank
{
    money o ; // embedded object
};
```

(b) Composition and containership is one and the same thing.

Ans

True.

(c) Composition and Inheritance both promote reuse of code.

Ans

True. The composition promotes reusability by creating an object of the existing class within another class. On the other hand inheritance promotes reusability by allowing a class to be derived from a base class.

(d) A function that is a *friend* of a class can access *private* data member of a class but cannot manipulate them.

Ans

False. This is shown in the following example:

```
#include <iostream.h>

class two ;
class one
{
    int i ;

    public :

        one ( int ii )
        {
            i = ii ;
        }

        friend int changedata ( one, two ) ;
};
class two
{
    int j ;

    public :

        two ( int jj )
        {
            j = jj ;
        }

        friend int changedata ( one, two ) ;
```

```
};

int changedata ( one a, two b )
{
    a.i = 100 ;
    return a.i + b.j ;
}

void main( )
{
    one  a ( 500 ) ;
    two  b ( 500 ) ;
    cout << changedata( a, b ) ;
}
```

Ans

The output of the program would be 600.

The *friend* function *changedata( )* is not only accessing the *private* data of the class *one* but also manipulating it.

(e) If an entire class is made a *friend* of another, then all the member functions of this class can access the *private* data member of the original class.

Ans

True. This is shown in the following example:

```
#include <iostream.h>

class sample ;

class test
{
    private :

            int i ;
```

```cpp
    public :

        test( )
        {
            i = 9 ;
        }

        friend  sample ;
};
class sample
{
    public :

        void fun1 ( test  t )
        {
            cout << endl << t.i ;
        }

        void fun2 ( test  t )
        {
            cout << endl << t.i ;
        }
};
void main( )
{
    sample  s ;
    test  t ;
    s.fun1 ( t ) ;
    s.fun2 ( t ) ;
}
```

Ans

Here, class *sample* is a *friend* of class *test*. Hence we can easily access the *private* data members of the class *test* inside the class *sample*.

i is a *private* data member of the class *test* but it is accessible inside the member functions *fun1( )* and *fun2( )* of class *sample*, as class *sample* has been defined as a *friend* of the *test* class.

(f) Unless you have the source code of the class you cannot make the declaration of the *friend* function inside that class.

Ans

True.

(g) Using a smart pointer we can iterate through a container.

Ans

True. A container is a collection of elements or objects. It helps to properly organize and store the data. Stacks, linked lists, arrays are examples of containers.

Following program shows how to iterate through a container using a smart pointer.

```
#include <iostream.h>

class smartpointer
{
    private :

        int *p ;  // ordinary pointer

    public :

        smartpointer ( int  n )
        {
            p = new int [ n ] ;
            int *t = p ;
            for ( int  i = 0 ; i <= 9 ; i++ )
                *t++ = i * i ;
```

```
                }

                int* operator ++ ( int )
                {
                        return p++ ;
                }

                int operator * ( )
                {
                        return *p ;
                }
        };

        void main( )
        {
            smartpointer  sp ( 10 ) ;

            for ( int  i = 0 ; i <= 9 ; i++ )
                cout << *sp++ << endl ;
        }
```

Here, *sp* is a smart pointer. When we say **sp*, the *operator * ( )* function gets called. It returns the integer being pointed to by *p*. When we say *sp++* the *operator ++ ( )* function gets called. It increments *p* to point to the next element in the array and then returns the address of this new location.

(h) Using a smart pointer we can make an object appear like a pointer.

Ans

True. If a class overloads the operator -> then any object of that class can appear like a pointer when the *operator -> ( )* is called. This is shown in the following example:

```
#include <iostream.h>
```

```
class test
{
    public :

        void fun( )
        {
            cout << "fun of smart pointer" ;
        }
} ;

class smartpointer
{
    test  t ;

    public :

        test* operator ->( )
        {
            return &t ;
        }

} ;

void main( )
{
    smartpointer  sp ;
    sp -> fun( ) ;
}
```

The beauty of overloading operator -> is that even though *sp* is an object, we can make it work like a pointer. The *operator -> ( )* returns the address of the object of the type *test*. Using this the function *fun( )* of the class *test* gets called. Thus even though *fun( )* is not a member of *smartpointer* class, we can still call it using *sp*.

(i)   The overloaded *operator ->* is called a smart pointer operator.

Ans

True. Refer (h) above.

(j) The pointer to member operator can be used to access particular data members within a class.

Ans

True. This is shown in the following example:

```
#include <iostream.h>

class sample
{
    public :

        sample ( int  ii, float  ff )
        {
            i = ii ;
            f = ff ;
        }

        int  i ;
        float  f ;
} ;

int  sample::*p1 = &sample::i ;
float  sample::*p2 = &sample::f ;

void main( )
{
    sample  s ( 25, 42.273f ) ;
    cout << s.*p1 << endl << s.*p2 ;
}
```

Here, *p1* and *p2* are pointers to data members *i* and *f* respectively. Using these pointers we can access the data members *i* and *f*. Note that we can use the pointer to data members for any object of type *sample*.

(k) Pointers to members are not tied with any specific object.

Ans

True. Consider a class *sample* containing the data member *i*. The pointer to data member *i* is defined as follows:

```
int sample::*p = &sample::i ;
```

sample:: indicates that *p* is pointer to member of the class *sample*. This pointer is initialized with *&sample::i*.

Actually there is no "address of" *sample::i* because we are referring to a class and not to an object of that class. *&sample::i* merely produces an offset into the class. The actual address would be produced when we combine that offset with the starting address of a particular object.

Hence *&sample::i* is nothing more than the syntax of pointer to member. If we use *p* with one object we would get one value, if we use it with another object we would get another value.

This shows that the pointers to members are not tied with any specific object.

(l) A *namespace* definition can be continued over multiple header files.

Ans

True. The following code snippet shows this:

```
// file1.h

namespace myname
{
    class sample1
```

```
    {
        // code
    };
}

// file2.h

namespace myname
{
    class sample2
    {
        // code
    };
}
```

The classes *sample1* and *sample2* are defined within the same *namespace myname* but present in two different header files.

When a *namespace* is continued in this manner, after its initial definition, the continuation is called an extension-namespace-definition.

Q 10.27

Write a program which has a class called *base*, with a virtual function defined in it. Derive two classes *derived1* and *derived2* from it. Store address of derived class objects into base class pointers. Using *typeid( )* and *dynamic_cast* identify the type of the object at run-time.

Ans

The following program shows this:

```
#include <typeinfo.h>
#include <iostream.h>

class base
{
    public :
```

```
        virtual void fun( )
        {
        }
};

class derived1 : public base
{
};

class derived2 : public base
{
};

void main( )
{
    derived1  d1, *pd1 = &d1 ;
    derived2  d2, *pd2 = &d2 ;
    base  *p1 = &d1, *p2 = &d2 ;

    if ( typeid ( *p1 ) == typeid ( *pd1 ) )
        cout << endl << "Of the same type" ;
    else
        cout << endl << "Not of the same type" ;

    if ( typeid ( *p2 ) == typeid ( *pd2 ) )
        cout << endl << "Of the same type" ;
    else
        cout << endl << "Not of the same type" ;

    if ( pd1 = dynamic_cast < derived1 * > ( p1 ) )
        cout << endl << "Of the type derived1" ;
    else
        cout << endl << "Not of the type derived1" ;

    if ( pd2 = dynamic_cast < derived2 * > ( p2 ) )
        cout << endl << "Of the type derived2" ;
    else
        cout << endl << "Not of the type derived2" ;
```

```
}
```

Q 10.28

Implement a stack using linked list. Using the smart pointer
concept add such a functionality to the class that the user would be
able to pop the data using the * operator. Using the -- operator the
node should get deleted and the top pointer should point to the
previous node.

Ans

Here is the program...

```cpp
#include <iostream.h>

class container
{
    private :

        struct node
        {
            int data ;
            node *link ;
        } *head, *current ;

        int count ;

    public :

        container( )
        {
            head = current = NULL ;
            count = 0 ;
        }

        void add ( int n )
        {
```

```
            node *temp = new node ;
            temp -> data = n ;
            temp -> link = NULL ;

            if ( head == NULL )
                head = current = temp ;
            else
            {
                node *q ;
                q = head ;

                while ( q -> link != NULL )
                    q = q -> link ;

                q -> link = temp ;
            }

            count++ ;
        }

        int getcount( )
        {
            return count ;
        }

        friend class smartpointer ;
} ;

class smartpointer
{
    private :

        container *cptr ;

    public :

        smartpointer ( container *t )
        {
```

```
            cptr = t ;
        }

        int operator *( )
        {
            if ( cptr -> current == NULL )
                return NULL ;
            else
            {
                int  i = cptr->current->data ;
                return i ;
            }
        }

        void operator --( )
        {
            container  temp ;
            temp.current = cptr -> current -> link ;

            if ( cptr -> current != NULL )
            {
                delete cptr -> current ;
                cptr -> current = temp.current ;
            }
        }
} ;

void main( )
{
    container  c ;

    c.add ( 10 ) ;
    c.add ( 30 ) ;
    c.add ( 0 ) ;
    c.add ( -40 ) ;
    c.add ( 50 ) ;

    smartpointer  sptr ( &c ) ;
```

```
    for ( int  i = 0 ; i < c.getcount( ) ; i++ )
    {
        cout << endl << *sptr ;
        --sptr ;
    }
}
```

Q 10.29

Write a program that will convert an integer pointer into an integer and vice-versa.

Ans

```
#include <iostream.h>

void main( )
{
    int i = 65000 ;

    int *iptr = reinterpret_cast <int *> ( i ) ;
    cout << endl << iptr ;

    iptr++ ;
    cout << endl << iptr ;

    i = reinterpret_cast <int> ( iptr ) ;
    cout << endl << i ;

    i++ ;
    cout << endl << i ;
}
```

Q 10.30

Declare a class having the following data members:

```
char  name [ 20 ] ;
int  age ;
float  sal ;
```

Write a program to scan and print the values of the objects of this class using *cin* and *cout* in *main( )*.

Ans

This is shown in the following example:

```
#include <iostream.h>

class sample
{
        char  name [ 20 ] ;
        int  age ;
        float  sal ;

     public :

        friend ostream& operator << ( ostream& o, sample& s ) ;
        friend istream& operator >> ( istream& i, sample& s ) ;
} ;

ostream& operator << ( ostream& o, sample& s )
{
    o << s.name << " " << s.age << " " << s.sal ;
    return o ;
}

istream& operator >> ( istream& i, sample& s )
{
    i >> s.name >> s.age >> s.sal ;
    return i ;
}

void main( )
{
    sample  s ;
    cout << "Enter name, age and salary : " ;
    cin >> s ;
```

```
    cout << s ;
}
```

Templates

Q 11.1

What are templates?

Ans

Templates allow us to write one function or class that works for different data types. By using templates, we can design a single class/function that operates on many data types, instead of having to create a separate class/function for each type. When used with functions they are known as function *templates*, whereas when used with classes they are called class *templates*.

Q 11.2

When should we use templates?

Ans

Templates are often used to:

- Create a type-safe collection class (for example, a stack) that can operate on data of any type.

- Add extra type checking for functions that would otherwise take void pointers.

These tasks can be done even without using templates. However, using templates offers several advantages:

- Templates are easier to write. We can create only one generic version of our class or function instead of manually creating specific classes and functions.
- Templates can be easier to understand, since they can provide a straightforward way of abstracting type information.
- Templates are type-safe. Since the types that templates act upon are known at compile-time, the compiler can perform type checking before errors occur.

Q 11.3

Do templates provide reusability?

Ans

Yes, but of a different type. Templates provide a way to reuse the source code. Templates allow us to write one function or class that works for different data types. This significantly reduces source code size and increases code flexibility.

Q 11.4

Can we use templates for user-defined data types?

Ans

Yes. This is shown in the following example:

```
#include <iostream.h>

class test
{
    private :
```

```
            int i ;
            float j ;

        public :

            void display( )
            {
                cout << i << endl << j << endl ;
            }
};

class test1
{
    private :

            int x ;
            float y ;
            char ch ;

    public :

            void display( )
            {
                cout << x << endl << y << endl << ch << endl ;
            }
};

template <class T>
class sample
{
    private :

            T t ;

    public :

            void show( )
            {
```

```
            t.display( ) ;
        }
} ;

void main( )
{
    sample <test> s1 ;
    s1.show( ) ;

    sample <test1> s2 ;
    s2.show( ) ;
}
```

When we create object *s1* or *s2* from the class template *sample*, classes would get created containing either a data member of type *test* or *test1*.

Q 11.5

How does a template work?

Ans

At compile time the compiler simply remembers the function/class template for future use. For functions the actual code is generated when the function is called with a specific data type. As against this, classes are born while creating an object using the template arguments.

Q 11.6

What is the difference between the function template and template function?

Ans

Consider the following code snippet:

```
template <class T>
T max ( T  a, T  b )
{
    return ( a > b ) ? a : b ;
}
```

This entire syntax is called a function *template*. In a function template a data type is represented by a name (T in our case), it can be any other name as well. T here is known as template argument.

When the function is called, its code gets generated. This is called instantiating the function *template*. Each instantiated version of function is called a *template* function.

Q 11.7

What are the advantages of templates over macros?

Ans

Let us take an example, where we want to find the minimum of two values. For this the macro definition would be,

```
# define  min( i, j )  ( ( i ) < ( j ) ? ( i ) : ( j ) )
```

and its parallel template would be:

```
template <class T>
T min ( T  i, T  j )
{
    return ( ( i < j ) ? i : j ) ;
}
```

The macro given above performs a simple text substitution and can thus work with any type. However it suffers from several limitations:

- There is no way for the compiler to verify that the macro parameter is for compatible types. The macro is expanded without any special type checking.
- The type of the value returned isn't specified, so the compiler can't tell if we are assigning it to an incompatible variable.
- In the macro, the parameters *i* and *j* are evaluated twice. If either parameter has a post-incremented variable, the increment would take place twice.
- When the preprocessor expands the macros, the compiler error messages would refer to the expanded macro, rather than the macro definition itself. This makes bug hunting difficult.

By using templates we can overcome all these disadvantages.

Q 11.8

When is a class template instantiated?

Ans

Class templates are instantiated by defining an object using the template arguments. This is shown in the following example:

```
template <class T>
class sample
{
    // code
};

void main( )
{
    sample <int> s1 ;
    sample <float> s2 ;
    sample <char> s3 ;
}
```

When the object *s1*, *s2* and *s3* are instantiated, the class template is instantiated for each type and hence three different versions of class *sample* are created.

Q 11.9

Write the definition of member function of template class that is defined outside the class. The function receives a parameter of its own type and returns the value of the same type.

Ans

```
sample <T> sample<T>::fun ( sample  s )
{
    // code
}
```

Here, the first *sample<T>*, indicates the return type of the function and the next *sample<T>::* is used for the scope of function.

Q 11.10

Can we save the reproduction of code that does not depend on any type, while using the template?

Ans

Yes. Every time we instantiate a template the code in the template is generated anew. If some of the functionality of a template does not depend on type, it can be put in a common base class to prevent unnecessary reproduction of that code. The following code snippet shows this.

```
class test
{
    // code common for all the data types
};


template <class T>
class sample : public test
{
    // code
};
```

Q 11.11

Consider the following two files:

```
// temp.h
template <class T>
void fun ( T x, T y ) ;

// temp.cpp
template <class T>
void fun ( T x, T y )
{
    // code
}
```

The file "temp.h" contains the declaration of a template function *fun( )* and the file "temp.cpp" contains its definition. Would the following program work?

```
// main.cpp
#include "temp.h"

void main( )
{
    int i, j ;
    fun ( i, j ) ;
}
```

Ans

No. For a template function to work it is mandatory that its definition should always be present in the same file from where it is called. This is because the programs that are present in different files are compiled separately, even if the files are present in the same project.

In the above program the template function *fun( )* is present in "temp.cpp", and merely including the file "temp.h" which contains its declaration is not enough. When its time to compile the template function *fun( )*, the compiler is unable to decide as to which particular version of function should it create. So it creates the template version which is of no use for any data type. Hence while calling the function *fun( )* for any data type it results into a linker error.

Q 11.12

State whether the following statements are True or False:

(a) If there is a function template called *max( )* then a specific version of it would be created when *max( )* is called with a new type.

Ans

True. Call to the function *max( )* is resolved at compile time. When any data type (for e.g. *int*) is passed to the function *max( )*, the compiler will generate the specific version of the *max( )* function for that particular data type (i.e. for *int*). This process is often known as instantiating the function template.

When the function is called again but this time with some other data type (for e.g. *float*) then compiler will generate one more version of this function for the respective data type (i.e. for *float*).

(b) The compiler generates only one version of function template for each data type irrespective of the number of calls that are made for that type.

Ans

True. When any data type is passed to the function for the first time the compiler generates a version of function for that particular data type. Thereafter whenever the function is called for this particular data type the compiler calls the already generated version of the function for this data type.

(c) Using templates saves memory.

Ans

False. When template is used in a program it only saves the writing effort on programmer's part. Compiler anyway generates different versions of the code for different data types.

(d) We can override a function template for a particular type.

Ans

True. Usually we override a function template when we want different code to be executed for a particular data type. Following program shows how to override a function template.

```cpp
#include <iostream.h>

void fun ( float  a )
{
    cout << "float " ;
}

template <class  T>
void fun ( T  a )
{
    cout << "all in one" << endl ;
}

void main( )
{
    int  a = 10 ;
    fun ( a ) ;

    float  x = 25.09f ;
    fun ( x ) ;
}
```

The output of the program would be:

all in one
float

It clearly shows that the function *fun( )* which receives the parameter as float, overrides the function template *fun( )*.

(e) We cannot inherit a new class from the class template.

Ans

False. The syntax of deriving a new class from the class template is shown in the following example:

```
#include <iostream.h>

template <class  T>
class sample
{
    public :

        void fun ( T  i )
        {
            cout << i << endl ;
        }
} ;

template <class  Z>
class test : public sample <Z>
{
    public :

        void fun1 ( Z  i )
        {
            cout << i ;
        }
} ;
```

```
void main( )
{
    test <int> d ;
    d.fun ( 25 ) ;
    d.fun1 ( 9 ) ;
}
```

Here, class *test* is derived from the base class *sample*.

(f) A function template can have multiple argument types.

Ans

True. The following program shows such a function template.

```
#include <iostream.h>

template <class T, class S, class Z>
void fun ( T a, S b, Z c )
{
    cout << a << endl << b << endl << c ;
}

void main( )
{
    int  i = 10 ;
    float j = 3.14f ;
    char ch = 'A' ;

    fun ( i, j, ch ) ;
}
```

(g) Templates are type safe whereas macros are not.

Ans

True. When the call is resolved for a function template type checking is done, whereas, macros are expanded without type checking.

(h) Class templates are normally used for container class.

Ans

True. Containers such as stacks and linked lists are used to store data but can store only one type of data at a time. To store different types of data we are required to write different versions of the same container class. We can save this repetition of code by writing the class template.

(i) A class template member function can be defined outside the class template.

Ans

True. This is shown in the following example:

```
template <class T>
class sample
{
    public :

        void fun ( T  x ) ;
};

template <class T>
void sample<T>:: fun ( T  x )
{
    // code
}

void main( )
{
```

```
            sample  <int>  s ;
            s.fun ( 25 ) ;
      }
```

(j)   Template arguments can take default values.

Ans

True. The values of these arguments then become compile-time constants for that particular instantiation of the template. For example:

```
#include <iostream.h>

template <class  T, int  y = 50 >
class sample
{
     T  arr [ y ] ;

     public :

          void fun ( T  x, int  index )
          {
                arr [ index ] = x ;
                cout << arr [ index ] ;
          }
} ;

void main( )
{
     sample < float, 7 > s ;
     s.fun ( 9.521f, 2 ) ;
}
```

Here, we are passing a float and a constant integer value 7 as arguments to class template. Had we not passed 7, then 50 would have been considered as the default value.

(k) Every formal parameter in the template definition must appear at least once in the function's parameter list.

Ans

True.

(l) Formal parameter names must be unique in the parameter list of a function template.

Ans

False. We can have formal parameters with the same name. This is shown in the following example:

```
#include <iostream.h>

template <class T>
void fun ( T  i, T  j )
{
    T  k ;
    k = i + j ;
    cout << k ;
}

void main( )
{
    fun ( 8, 12 ) ;
}
```

(m) A function template can be overloaded.

Ans

True. A function template can be overloaded only if the number of formal arguments is different. Overloading of function template is invalid if the number of arguments is same. This is shown in the following example:

```
#include <iostream.h>

template <class T>
void fun ( T i, T j )
{
    cout << i << endl << j << endl ;
}

template <class T>
void fun ( T i )
{
    cout << i ;
}

void main( )
{
    fun ( 8, 12 ) ;
    fun ( 25 ) ;
}
```

(n) Actual code for the function template is generated when the function is called.

Ans

True. A function template can be called with different data types. Till the call is not made it is not clear to the compiler as to which version of the function should be generated. This becomes clear when the function is called with a particular data type. Hence actual code for the function template is generated after the call is made.

(o) We can distribute function templates and class templates in object libraries.

Ans

False. We can compile a function template or a class template into object code (.obj file). The code that contains a call to the function template or the code that creates an object from a class template can get compiled. This is because the compiler merely checks whether the call matches the declaration (in case of function template) and whether the object definition matches class declaration (in case of class template). Since the function template and the class template definitions are not found, the compiler leaves it to the linker to restore this. However, during linking, linker doesn't find the matching definitions for the function call or a matching definition for object creation. In short the expanded versions of templates are not found in the object library. Hence the linker reports errors.

Q 11.13

Write a program that will implement a binary tree as a class template.

Ans

```
#include <iostream.h>

#define FALSE 0
#define TRUE 1

template <class  T>
class tree
{
    private :

        struct node
        {
            node *l ;
            T  data ;
            node *r ;
```

```
        } *p ;

    public :

        tree ( ) ;
        void search ( T  n, int  &found, node*  &parent ) ;
        void in ( node  *q ) ;
        void pre ( node  *q ) ;
        void post ( node  *q ) ;
        int compare ( node  *pp, node  *qq ) ;
        node* copy ( node  *q ) ;
        void insert ( T  n ) ;
        void traverse ( ) ;
        int operator == ( tree  t ) ;
        void operator = ( tree  t ) ;
} ;

template <class  T>
tree<T>::tree( )
{
    p = NULL ;
}

template <class  T>
void tree<T>::search ( T  n, int  &found, node*  &parent )
{
    node *q ;
    found = FALSE ;
    parent = NULL ;

    if ( p == NULL )
        return ;
    q = p ;

    while ( q != NULL )
    {
        if ( q -> data == n )
        {
```

```
                found = TRUE ;
                return ;
            }

        if ( q -> data > n )
        {
            parent = q ;
            q = q -> l ;
        }
        else
        {
            parent = q ;
            q = q -> r ;
        }
    }
}

template <class  T>
void tree<T>::in ( node  *q )
{
    if ( q != NULL )
    {
        in ( q -> l ) ;
        cout << '\t' << q -> data ;
        in ( q -> r ) ;
    }
}

template <class  T>
void tree<T>::pre ( node  *q )
{
    if ( q != NULL )
    {
        cout << '\t' << q -> data ;
        pre ( q -> l ) ;
        pre ( q -> r ) ;
    }
}
```

```cpp
template <class T>
void tree<T>::post ( node *q )
{
    if ( q != NULL )
    {
        post ( q -> l ) ;
        post ( q -> r ) ;
        cout << '\t' << q -> data ;
    }
}

template <class T>
int tree<T>::compare ( node *pp, node *qq )
{
    static int flag ;
    if ( ( ( pp==NULL ) && ( qq == NULL ) )
        flag = TRUE ;
    else
    {
        if ( ( ( pp != NULL ) && ( qq != NULL ) )
        {
            if ( pp -> data != qq -> data )
                flag = FALSE ;
            else
            {
                compare ( pp -> l, qq -> r ) ;
                compare ( qq -> l, qq -> r ) ;
            }
        }
    }
    return ( flag ) ;
}

template <class T>
tree<T>::node* tree<T>::copy ( node *q )
{
    node *t ;
    if ( q != NULL )
```

```
        {
            t = new node ;
            t -> data = q -> data ;
            t -> l = copy ( q -> l ) ;
            t -> r = copy ( q -> r ) ;
            return ( t ) ;
        }
        else
            return ( NULL ) ;
}

template <class  T>
void tree<T>::insert ( T  n )
{
        int  found ;
        node *t , *parent ;
        search ( n, found, parent ) ;
        if ( found == TRUE )
            cout << endl << "Such a node already exist" ;
        else
        {
            t = new node ;
            t -> data = n ;
            t -> l = NULL ;
            t -> r = NULL ;

            if ( parent == NULL )
                p = t ;
            else
                parent -> data > n ? parent ->l = t :parent -> r = t ;
        }
}

template <class  T>
void tree<T> :: traverse ( )
{
        int  choice ;
        cout << endl << "1. Inorder" ;
```

```
        cout << endl << "2. Preorder" ;
        cout << endl << "3. Postorder" ;
        cout << endl << "Your Choice" ;
        cin >> choice ;

        switch ( choice )
        {
        case 1 :
            in ( p ) ;
            break ;
        case 2 :
            pre ( p ) ;
            break ;
        case 3 :
            post ( p ) ;
            break ;
        }
}

template <class T>
int tree<T>::operator == ( tree<T> t )
{
        int  flag ;
        flag = compare ( p, t.p ) ;
        return ( flag ) ;
}

template <class  T>
void tree<T>::operator = ( tree<T>  t )
{
        p = copy ( t.p ) ;
}

void main( )
{
        tree <int> tt ;
        tree <int> ss ;
        int  i, num ;
```

```
for ( i = 0 ; i <= 6 ; i++  )
{
     cout << endl << "Enter the data for the node to be inserted " ;
     cin >> num ;
     tt.insert ( num ) ;
}

tt.traverse( ) ;
ss = tt ;
ss.traverse( ) ;

if ( ss == tt )
     cout << endl << "Tree Are Equal" ;
else
     cout << endl << "tree are Unequal " ;

cout << endl << "Tree for float values" ;

tree <float> ft ;
tree <float> fs ;
float  num1 ;

for ( i = 0 ; i <= 6 ; i++  )
{
     cout << endl << "Enter the data for the node to be inserted " ;
     cin >> num1 ;
     ft.insert ( num1 ) ;
}

ft.traverse( ) ;
fs = ft ;
fs.traverse( ) ;

if ( fs == ft )
     cout << endl << "Tree Are Equal" ;
else
     cout << endl << "tree are Unequal " ;
}
```

Q 11.14

Write a program to implement a doubly linked list as a class template.

Ans

```cpp
#include <iostream.h>

template <class T>
class linklist
{
    private :

        struct node
        {
            node *prev ;
            T  data ;
            node *next ;
        } *p ;

    public :

        linklist( ) ;
        ~linklist( ) ;
        void append ( T ) ;
        void addatbeg ( T ) ;
        void addafter ( int , T ) ;
        void deletenode ( T ) ;
        void display( ) ;
        int count ( ) ;
} ;

template <class  T>
linklist<T>::linklist( )
{
    p = NULL ;
}
```

```
template <class T>
linklist<T>::~linklist( )
{
    node *t ;
    while ( p!= NULL )
    {
        t = p ;
        p = p -> next ;
        delete t ;
    }
}

template <class T>
void linklist<T>::append ( T num )
{
    node *q, *t ;
    q = p ;
    if ( q == NULL )
    {
        q = new node ;
        q -> prev = NULL ;
        q -> data = num ;
        q -> next = NULL ;
        p = q ;
    }
    else
    {
        while ( q -> next != NULL )
            q = q -> next ;

        t = new node ;
        t -> prev = q ;
        t -> data = num ;
        t -> next = NULL ;
        q -> next = t ;
    }
}
```

```
template <class T>
void linklist<T>::addatbeg ( T num )
{
    node *q ;
    q = new node ;
    q -> prev = NULL ;
    q -> data = num ;
    q -> next = p ;
    p -> prev = q ;
    p = q ;
}

template <class T>
void linklist<T>::addafter ( int loc, T num )
{
    node *t, *q ;
    q = p ;
    for ( int i = 0 ; i <= loc ; i++ )
    {
        q = q -> next ;
        if ( q == NULL )
        {
            cout << endl << "There are less than "<< loc <<"element" ;
            return ;
        }
    }

    q = q -> prev ;
    t = new node ;
    t -> data = num ;
    t -> prev = q ;
    t -> next = q -> next ;
    t -> next -> prev = t ;
    q -> next = t ;
}

template <class T>
void linklist<T>::deletenode ( T num )
```

```
{
    node  *q = p ;
    //traverse the entire list
    while ( q != NULL )
    {
        // if node to be deleted is found
        if ( q -> data == num )
        {
            if ( q == p )
            {
                p = p -> next ;
                p -> prev = NULL ;
            }
            else
            {
                if ( q -> next == NULL )
                    q -> prev -> next = NULL ;
                else
                {
                    q -> prev -> next = q -> next ;
                    q -> next -> prev = q -> prev ;
                }

                delete q ;
            }
            return ;
        }
        q = q -> next ;
    }
}

template <class T>
void linklist<T>::display( )
{
    node  *q ;
    q = p ;
    cout << endl ;
```

```
        while ( q != NULL )
        {
            cout << endl << q -> data ;
            q = q -> next ;
        }
}

template <class  T>
int linklist<T>::count ( )
{
    node  *q ;
    int c = 0 ;
    q = p ;

    while ( q != NULL )
    {
        q = q -> next ;
        c++ ;
    }
    return c ;
}

void main( )
{
    linklist <int> l1 ;

    l1.append ( 11 ) ;
    l1.append ( 22 ) ;
    l1.display( ) ;

    l1.addatbeg ( 33 ) ;
    l1.addatbeg ( 44 ) ;
    l1.display( ) ;

    l1.addafter ( 1, 100 ) ;
    l1.addafter ( 2, 200 ) ;
    l1.display( ) ;
```

```
l1.deletenode ( 33 ) ;
l1.deletenode ( 44 ) ;

l1.display( ) ;
cout << "No. of elements in linklist = " <<l1.count( ) ;

linklist <float> l2 ;

l2.append ( 1.1f ) ;
l2.append ( 2.2f ) ;

l2.display( ) ;


l2.addatbeg ( 3.3f ) ;
l2.addatbeg ( 4.4f ) ;
l2.display( ) ;

l2.addafter ( 1, 10.10f ) ;
l2.addafter ( 2, 20.20f ) ;
l2.display( ) ;

l2.deletenode ( 3.3f ) ;
l2.deletenode ( 4.4f ) ;

l2.display( ) ;
cout << "No. of elements in linklist = " << l2.count( ) ;
}
```

Q 11.15

Write a program that implements a template-based quick sort.

Ans

```
#include <iostream.h>
#include <string.h>

class mystring
```

```
{
    private :

        enum { sz = 100 } ;
        char str [ sz ] ;

    public :

        mystring ( char *s = "" )
        {
            strcpy ( str, s ) ;
        }

        int operator < ( mystring  ss )
        {
            if ( strcmp ( str, ss.str ) <= 0 )
                return 1 ;
            else
                return 0 ;
        }

        int operator <= ( mystring  ss )
        {
            if ( strcmp ( str, ss.str ) <= 0 )
                return 1 ;
            else
                return 0 ;
        }

        int operator > ( mystring  ss )
        {
            if ( strcmp ( str, ss.str ) > 0 )
                return 1 ;
            else
                return 0 ;
        }

    friend ostream& operator << ( ostream &o, mystring &dd ) ;
```

```
};

ostream& operator << ( ostream  &o, mystring  &ss )
{
    o << ss.str ;
    return o ;
}

class date
{
    private :

        int  day, mth, yr ;

    public :

        date ( int  d = 0, int  m = 0, int  y = 0 )
        {
            day = d ;
            mth = m ;
            yr = y ;
        }

        int  operator < ( date  dt )
        {
            if ( yr < dt.yr )
                return 1 ;

            if ( yr == dt.yr && mth < dt.mth )
                return 1 ;

            if ( yr == dt.yr && mth == dt.mth && day < dt.day )
                return 1 ;

            return 0 ;
        }

        int  operator <= ( date  dt )
```

```
                {
                    if ( yr <= dt.yr )
                        return 1 ;

                    if ( yr == dt.yr && mth <= dt.mth )
                        return 1 ;

                    if ( yr == dt.yr && mth == dt.mth && day <= dt.day )
                        return 1 ;

                    return 0 ;
                }

                int operator > ( date dt )
                {
                    if ( yr > dt.yr )
                        return 1 ;

                    if ( yr == dt.yr && mth > dt.mth )
                        return 1 ;

                    if ( yr == dt.yr && mth == dt.mth && day > dt.day )
                        return 1 ;

                    return 0 ;
                }

                friend ostream& operator << ( ostream  &o, date  &dd ) ;
} ;

ostream& operator << ( ostream  &o, date  &dd )
{
    o << dd.day << "\t" << dd.mth << "\t" << dd.yr ;
    return o ;
}

template <class  T>
void quick ( T *n, int  low, int  high )
```

```
{
    int pos ;

    if ( low < high )
    {
        pos = split ( n, low, high ) ;
        quick ( n, low, pos - 1 ) ;
        quick ( n, pos + 1, high ) ;
    }
}

template <class T>
int split ( T *n, int low, int high )
{
    int pos, left, right ;
    T item, t ;

    item = n [ low ] ;
    left = low ;
    right = high ;

    while ( left < right )
    {
        while ( n [ right ] > item )
            right = right - 1 ;

        while ( ( left < right ) && ( n [ left ] <= item ) )
            left = left + 1 ;

        if ( left < right )
        {
            t = n [ left ] ;
            n[left] = n [ right ] ;
            n[right] = t ;
        }
    }

    pos = right ;
```

```
        t = n [ low ] ;
        n [ low ] = n [ pos ] ;
        n [ pos ] = t ;

        return pos ;
}

void main( )
{
        float  num[ ] = { 5.4f, 3.23f, 2.15f, 1.09f, 34.66f, 23.3452f } ;
        int  arr[ ] = { -12, 23, 14, 0, 245, 78 , 66, -9 } ;
        date  dtarr[ ] = { date ( 17, 11, 62 ), date ( 23, 12, 65 ), date ( 12, 12, 78 ),
                       date ( 23, 1, 69 ) } ;
        mystring  strarr[ ] = { mystring ( "Kamal" ), mystring ( "Anuj" ),
                            mystring ( "Sachin" ), mystring ( "Anil" ) } ;
        int  i ;
        cout << endl << endl ;
        quick ( num, 0, 5 ) ;
        for ( i = 0 ; i <= 5 ; i++ )
            cout << num [ i ] << endl ;

        cout << endl << endl ;
        quick ( arr, 0, 7 ) ;
        for ( i = 0 ; i <= 7 ; i++ )
            cout << arr [ i ] << endl ;

        cout << endl << endl ;
        quick ( dtarr, 0, 3 ) ;
        for ( i = 0 ; i <= 3 ; i++ )
            cout << dtarr [ i ] << endl ;

        cout << endl << endl ;
        quick ( strarr, 0, 3 ) ;
        for ( i = 0 ; i <= 3 ; i++ )
            cout << strarr [ i ] << endl ;
}
```

Exception Handling

Q 12.1

What are exceptions? Give some reasons that cause exceptions?

Ans

Exceptions are errors that occur at run-time. Following are the few reasons that can cause exceptions:

- Inability to open a file
- Exceeding the bounds of an array
- Attempting to initialize an object to an impossible value
- Falling short of memory

Q 12.2

How can we handle exceptions?

Ans

The exceptions are handled by using *try, throw* and *catch* blocks. The following code shows the organization of these blocks.

```
class sample
```

```
{
    public :

        // exception class
        class errorclass
        {
        } ;

        void fun( )
        {
            if ( some error occurs )
                throw errorclass( ) ;   // throws exception
        }
} ;

// application
void main( )
{
    // try block
    try
    {
        sample s ;
        s.fun( ) ;
    }
    catch ( sample :: errorclass )     // exception handler or catch block
    {
        // do something about the error
    }
}
```

Here *sample* is any class in which errors might occur. An exception class called *errorclass*, is specified in the *public* part of *sample*. This *errorclass* is the one that handles the error. In *main( )* we have enclosed part of the program that uses *sample* in a *try* block. If an error occurs in *sample::fun( )* we throw an exception, using the keyword *throw* followed by the constructor for the *errorclass*:

throw errorclass( ) ;

When an exception is thrown, control goes to the *catch* block that immediately follows the *try* block.

Q 12.3

What is an exception handler?

Ans

The *catch* block that handles the run-time error, is also known as exception handler. The catch block must appear just after the *try* block.

Q 12.4

How does exception-handling mechanism work?

Ans

There are four parts involved in the exception handling mechanism. These are as follows:

- Specifying the Exception Class
- Throwing an Exception
- The *try* Block
- The Exception Handler (*catch* Block)

Refer Q 12.2, for detailed explanation.

Q 12.5

If *stack* is a class that can throw an exception and *stackempty* is the exception class, then can we define the *catch* block in either of the following two ways:

— catch (stack ::stackempty)
— catch (stackempty)

Ans

It depends upon where the exception class *stackempty* is defined. If the exception class *stackempty* is defined in the public section of the class *stack*, then the first statement is correct and the second is wrong. If the exception class *stackempty* is defined outside the class *stack*, then the second statement is correct and the first one is wrong.

Q 12.6

Can we have exceptions that take arguments?

Ans

Yes. This is shown in the following program:

```cpp
#include <string.h>
#include <iostream.h>

class exception
{
    private :

        char  str [ 20 ] ;

    public :

        exception ( char  *p )
        {
            strcpy ( str, p ) ;
        }

        void cause( )
        {
            cout << str << endl ;
        }
} ;
```

```
class sample1
{
    public :

        void fun( )
        {
            throw exception ( "from sample1" ) ;
        }
} ;

class sample2
{
    public :

        void fun( )
        {
            throw exception ( "from sample2" ) ;
        }
} ;

void main( )
{
    try
    {
        sample1  s1 ;
        s1.fun( ) ;

        sample2  s2 ;
        s2.fun( ) ;
    }
    catch ( exception  e )
    {
        e.cause( ) ;
    }
}
```

Here *exception* is the exception class that contains a one-argument constructor. While throwing the exception a string is passed to its constructor specifying the class name from where the exception is thrown. When the *fun( )* function of the class *sample1* gets called an exception is thrown which is caught in the catch block. From the catch block a function *cause( )* is called which displays the class name from where the exception is thrown.

Note that the statements,

sample2 s2 ;
s2.fun( ) ;

would never work because exception is thrown before these statements in the same *try* block. When the exception occurs, the control jumps to the *catch* block, thereby skipping these statements.

Q 12.7

How would you write the exception specification for the following type of functions?

(a) Function that throws three types of exceptions

(b) Function that can throw any exception

Ans

The exception specifications of the functions are as follows:

(a)   void fun( ) throw (first, second, third)

(b)   void fun( )

Q 12.8

Do we have built-in exception classes?

Ans

Yes. Standard C++ contains several built-in exception classes. The most commonly used is probably *bad_alloc*, which is thrown if an error occurs when attempting to allocate memory with *new*.

Q 12.9

How to return an error value from the constructor?

Ans

We cannot return any error value from the constructor, as the constructor doesn't have any return type. However, by throwing an exception we can pass value to *catch* block. This is shown in the following example:

```
#include <iostream.h>

class sample
{
    public :

        sample ( int i )
        {
            if ( i == 0 )
                throw "error" ;
        }
} ;

void main( )
{
    try
    {
        sample s ( 0 ) ;
    }
    catch ( char * str )
    {
        cout << str ;
```

```
        }
}
```

Q 12.10

How to catch multiple types of exceptions in one single *catch* block?

Ans

This can be explained with the help of following example:

```cpp
#include <iostream.h>

class test
{
};

class sample
{
    public :

        void fun1( )
        {
            throw 99 ;
        }

        void fun2( )
        {
            throw 3.14f ;
        }

        void fun3( )
        {
            throw "error" ;
        }

        void fun4( )
        {
```

```
                throw test( ) ;
            }
};

void main( )
{
    try
    {
        sample  s ;
        s.fun4( ) ;
        s.fun1( ) ;
        s. fun2( ) ;
        s. fun3( ) ;
    }
    catch ( ... )
    {
        cout << "strange" ;
    }
}
```

Here, different types of exceptions are thrown by the member functions of the class *sample*. While catching the exception, instead of four different *catch* blocks we can as well define one single *catch* block. But the syntax for defining the *catch* block is we have to mention the three dots (…) in the formal parameter list. This indicates that any thrown exception is caught in the same *catch* block. Here when the exception is thrown from the *fun4( )* control reaches the *catch* block, ignoring the rest of the calls.

Q 12.11

State whether the following statements are True or False:

(a) The exception handling mechanism is supposed to handle compile time errors.

Ans

False. The exception handling mechanism is used to handle the run-time errors.

(b) It is always necessary to declare the exception class within the class in which an exception is going to be thrown.

Ans

False. The alternate way to declare the exception class is shown in the following example:

```
class fullorempty
{
} ;

class queue
{
    public :

            void addq ( int  item ) throw ( fullorempty )
            {
                // some code
            }

            int  delq( ) throw ( fullorempty )
            {
                // some code
            }
} ;

void main( )
{
    queue  a ;

    try
    {
        // some code
```

```
    }
    catch ( fullorempty  fe )
    {
        // some code
    }
}
```

Here *fullorempty* is the exception class that is declared outside the class *queue*. The following notification

```
void addq ( int  item ) throw ( fullorempty )
```

is known as exception specification.

(c) Every thrown exception must be caught.

Ans

False. If an exception is thrown and its matching exception handler is not provided then the program is terminated (unceremoniously) by the operating system.

(d) For one try block there can be multiple *catch* blocks.

Ans

True. There can be more than one exception handler (or *catch* block) for one *try* block, because it might so happen that in one single *try* block there can be different types of exceptions that can be thrown. This is shown in the following code snippet:

```
try
{
    // statement that throws divide-by-zero exception
    // statement that throws array out-of-bound exception
}
catch ( divide_error id1 )
{
```

```
        // code
    }
    catch ( out_of_bound_error id2 )
    {
        // code
    }
```

(e) The *catch* block and the exception handler are one and the same thing.

   Ans

   True.

(f) When an exception is thrown an exception class's constructor gets called.

   Ans

   True. We need an object of the exception class that will call the exception handler. So, when the exception is thrown, firstly the constructor of the exception class is called that creates an object of the exception class then the exception handler gets called.

(g) *try* blocks cannot be nested.

   Ans

   False.

(h) Proper destruction of an object is guaranteed by exception handling mechanism.

Ans

True. When an exception is thrown, a destructor is called automatically for any object that was created by the code up to that point in the *try* block.

(i) In a program if there is a possibility of an exception then it is necessary to write all the statements in the *try* block.

Ans

False. Exception can be handled successfully even if in the *try* block we write only the statement that may throw an exception.

Q 12.12

What will be the output of the following program?

```
#include <iostream.h>

class excep
{
};

class excep1 : public excep
{
};

class sample
{
    public :

        void fun( )
        {
            throw excep1( );
        }
};

void main( )
```

```
{
    try
    {
        sample s ;
        s.fun( ) ;
    }
    catch ( excep e1 )
    {
        cout << "excep" ;
    }
    catch ( excep1 e2 )
    {
        cout << "excep1" ;
    }
}
```

Ans

The output would be:

excep

Here the exception class *excep1* is derived from the exception class *excep*. When the function *fun( )* throws an exception of the class *excep1*, it is caught by the first *catch* block. This is because the nameless object of class *excep1* which is thrown from the function *fun( )* gets sliced when collected as an argument in the first *catch* block.

On the other hand, had we exchanged the positions of the two *catch* blocks, then class *excep1 catch* block would have been able to catch the exception.

Hence in our program the compiler gives a warning,

"class *excep1* is already caught by base class, class *excep*". Hence there is no need to define the class *excep1 catch* block.

Q 12.13

Implement an exception handling mechanism which reports stack full and stack empty mechanism for a class called *stack*.

Ans

```
#include <iostream.h>
#define MAX 4

class stack
{
    private :

        int  arr [ MAX ] ;
        int  top ;

    public :

        stack( )
        {
            top = -1  ;
        }

        class stackfull
        {
        } ;

        class stackempty
        {
        } ;

        void push ( int  item )
        {
            if ( top == MAX - 1 )
                throw stackfull( ) ;

            top++ ;
            arr [ top ] = item ;
```

```
        }

        int pop ( )
        {
            if ( top == -1 )
                throw stackempty( ) ;

            int  data = arr [ top ] ;
            top-- ;
            return data ;
        }
};

void main( )
{
    stack  s ;

    try
    {
        s.push ( 11 ) ;
        s.push ( 12 ) ;
        s.push ( 13 ) ;
        s.push ( 14 ) ;
        s.push ( 15 ) ;
        s.push ( 16 ) ;
    }
    catch ( stack::stackfull )
    {
        cout << endl << "Stack is full" ;
    }

    try
    {
        int  i = s.pop( ) ;
        cout << endl << "Item popped=" << i ;
        i = s.pop( ) ;
        cout << endl << "Item popped=" << i ;
        i = s.pop( ) ;
```

```
            cout << endl << "Item popped=" << i ;
            i = s.pop( ) ;
            cout << endl << "Item popped=" << i ;
            i = s.pop( ) ;
            cout << endl << "Item popped=" << i ;
    }
    catch ( stack ::stackempty )
    {
            cout << endl << "Stack is empty" ;
    }
}
```

Q 12.14

Create a class with its own *operator new*. This operator should allocate 5 objects, and on 5th 'run out of memory' and throw an exception. Also add a *static* member function that reclaims this memory. Create *main( )* with a *try* block and a *catch* block that calls the memory-restoration routine. Put this inside a *while* loop to demonstrate recovering from an exception and continuing execution.

Ans

```
#include <malloc.h>
#include <iostream.h>

class sample
{
    private :

        static int  count ;

    public :

        class nonew
        {
        } ;
```

```
void* operator new ( size_t  sz )
{
    if ( count == 4 )
    {
        count = 0 ;
        throw nonew( ) ;
    }
    count++ ;
    sample *ss = ( sample * ) malloc ( sz ) ;
    return ss ;
}

static void reclaim ( sample *s )
{
    delete  s ;
}
} ;

int sample::count = 0 ;

void main( )
{
    sample *s [ 5 ] ;

    while ( 1 )
    {
        try
        {
            for ( int i = 0 ; i <= 4 ; i++ )
                s [ i ] = new sample ;
        }
        catch ( sample::nonew )
        {
            for ( int i = 0 ; i <= 3 ; i++ )
                sample::reclaim ( s [ i ] ) ;
        }
    }
}
```

Index

B

C

G

O